Time and Workplace

Management
for Lawyers

Dr. Amy L. Jarmon

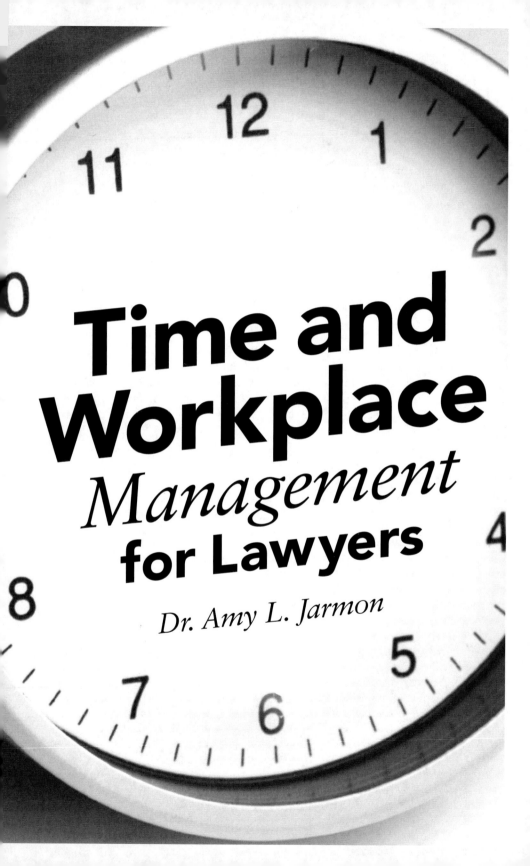

Time and Workplace
Workplace
Management
for Lawyers

Dr. Amy L. Jarmon

Cover and page layout by Monica Alejo/ABA Publishing.

Printed in the United States of America.

17 16 15 14 13   5 4 3 2

Library of Congress Cataloging-in-Publication Data

Jarmon, Amy L.
Time and workplace management for lawyers/Amy L. Jarmon.
    pages cm
Includes bibliographical references and index.
ISBN 978-1-61438-908-8 (alk. paper)
1. Lawyers—Time management—United States. I. Title.
KF315.J37 2013
650.1'102434--dc23
                    2013009046

Discounts are available for books ordered in bulk. Special consideration is given to state bars, CLE programs, and other bar-related organizations. Inquire at Book Publishing, ABA Publishing, American Bar Association, 321 North Clark Street, Chicago, Illinois 60654-7598.

www.ShopABA.org

Dedication

To my father, Franklin B. Jarmon, who taught me everything I value about the dignity of hard work, integrity, respect for others, and living out one's faith on a daily basis.

Table of Contents

Preface

Throughout my years in higher education administration and the practice of law, I have been interested in time management and work management strategies. I have implemented a multitude of different techniques and modified them to fit new work environments as I changed jobs and careers. With the impact of technology on the world of work, I learned how to embrace the positives of technology and deal with the negatives.

From all these varied experiences, I have learned three things about time and work management:

- One has to adopt strategies in stages. It is not possible to solve all of one's time and work management problems overnight. It takes persistence to implement new strategies that cumulatively make all the difference.
- One has to adapt strategies to the specific work environment. What works well in one situation might not in another. What pleases one supervisor might not be embraced by another.
- One can use time and work management strategies effectively to retain a personal life even though the legal profession seems to demand so much time.

I would like to thank several outstanding supervisors for teaching me so much about time and work management strategies, supervision and delegation, and the work-life balance that we all need: W. Samuel Sadler, Rodney C. Kelchner, Sir J. Anthony Holland, and Elizabeth A. Reilly.

There were many colleagues and friends who offered insights and support during the writing of this book. I especially want to thank Wes Cochran, Kay Fletcher, and Pam Dawkins for their ongoing support through this long process. Thank you to Joel Cook, Gilda McDowell, Lezlie Olibas, and Lindsay Olibas-Yanez for sharing their experiences. Grateful thanks go to my brother, Randall Jarmon, who reviewed a draft and offered many helpful comments. Special thanks to Bonnie Stepleton and Dennis Tonsing for their insightful suggestions.

Introduction

The daily workload of a lawyer includes multiple projects, competing deadlines, and unexpected crises. Without good strategies to manage the demands, a lawyer can become overwhelmed by the fast pace of law practice. Too many lawyers cope with their workloads by just spending longer hours at the office. They settle into a survival mentality that is highly stressful and personally unrewarding.

The purpose of this book is to provide strategies that will help you gain control over your professional life so that you can still have a fulfilling personal life outside the office. These pages contain practical advice for making time and work management decisions that will lead you to become more productive during your workday.

This book is written for both new lawyers with minimal work experience as well as lawyers who have practiced for several years and want to become more productive. The main headings and subheadings within the text are meant to help you determine which sections will be most useful given your own expertise with time and work management strategies. Choose the sections you need and skip the sections that speak to areas in which you are already proficient.

There will be some intentional repetition throughout the book because some ideas carry over into several topics or need to be reemphasized. The diversity within the legal profession as to size of employer, type of legal practice, use of technology, and sophistication of practice management defy a one-size-fits-all book. A middle-ground approach has been taken to encompass the most typical characteristics of legal employers. Although the legal workplace throughout the book will be designated generically by a "law firm" descriptor, all the strategies are relevant to any legal employer's environment. Some additional material specifically relevant to non-firm lawyers and to solo practitioners will be addressed in Chapters 11 and 12, respectively.

General Observations

Before we get into specific techniques, we need to consider several general observations about time and work management. These observations will help you gain the perspective needed to implement the strategies in this book more quickly as you organize your time and work.

Time is a limited resource that can be used wisely or frittered away. Everyone has the same 168 hours each week to accomplish professional and personal goals. Lawyers who organize their time and tasks carefully will be more successful at meeting their professional obligations while still having personal time.

Implement the strategies in this book in stages. If you try to change too many things at once, you will overwhelm yourself. Choose a few of the easier techniques to implement first. Those successful techniques will provide you with the incentive to implement more techniques. As you gain momentum, select techniques that may be more challenging but will have the greatest impact on your productivity and quality of life.

You will never just *find* time to complete all the projects on your desk. You need to *make* time for completing tasks. You need to structure your hours and your workload intentionally. Otherwise, you will be no closer at 7:00 p.m. to finishing the project you meant to start at 7:00 a.m.

You must work toward being more efficient and effective in *everything* you do. Efficiency is about using each minute wisely. Effectiveness is about getting the most results from your time. By increasing both efficiency and effectiveness, you will become more productive in less time.

You must set reasonable boundaries because you cannot be all things to all people. Your internal motivation to produce excellent work for your clients is essential to your success. It is humanly impossible, however, to do everything that everyone asks of you at the exact moment it is requested. Without reasonable boundaries on your time and work, you will spread yourself too thin, the quality of your work product will suffer, and you will pay the price in stress and exhaustion.

Learn to prioritize tasks. Learn to negotiate realistic deadlines. Learn to say "not right now" or no as appropriate.

You must have a plan to deal with the interruptions, conflicting demands, and unexpected events in your day. Rarely does a lawyer have the luxury of a day that runs exactly as desired. However, you can adopt strategies to limit the chaos so that your day is impacted minimally. If you know how to handle the unexpected, you can stay in control rather than be overwhelmed.

Know Your Legal Environment

Each legal job has its own idiosyncrasies and rhythm. Each legal employer has its unique culture and policies. The basic characteristics of your workplace will influence every decision you make about your time and work management. By evaluating your legal environment carefully, you will be well positioned to determine which of the strategies in this book can be implemented immediately, which will need to be modified, and which may need to be deferred until later.

How many areas of law do you practice? It is often said that a new lawyer needs three to five years to feel completely secure in a practice area. Those who have multiple specialty areas to cover for the firm will need to be more adept at mastering new material in different legal fields while juggling daily work obligations. Once knowledgeable in their areas, lawyers still need to allocate regular time to stay up to date. Although employers understand the need for lawyers to gain expertise and stay current, they expect high productivity at all times. Possessing time and work management skills will help you carve out time for your initial mastery of the law and continued study later while still completing your daily work.

Are there more-seasoned lawyers in your legal specialty within the firm that can assist you? Having colleagues available for assistance can save you time when you are confronted with a new legal problem. In large and mid-sized firms, you may have several colleagues in your practice area that can answer questions, indicate procedures, and generally advise you on client files. In a very small firm, you may find that you have been hired to replace the firm's only specialist in your area of law; however, seasoned colleagues can still give you some guidance. If you are a solo practitioner without colleagues to assist you, then you will need to structure time in your schedule to cultivate mentors.

Are you responsible for your own client files, other lawyers' files, or a combination? If you handle other lawyers' files, the work may be assigned unexpectedly without consideration for your other projects and deadlines. Another challenge is that the instructions for your narrow assignment may provide you with minimal context on the overall client matter. You will need to organize your work so that you can not only gain any context you need but also fit the project in with other deadlines. If you are running your own client files, you will be intimately familiar with every aspect of each file and have control over the scheduling of each task.

Who in the firm has supervision over your work? Your supervisor's preferences will influence the time and work management routines you implement. Your goal will be to consistently meet or exceed your supervisor's expectations.

Ideally you want just one supervisor to report to in your firm. Even with one direct supervisor, however, you may still be assigned work from additional lawyers. With multiple sources of work, conflict over deadlines or priorities is likely to occur.

If you cover several practice areas, you will typically have a supervisor for each area. Different supervisors may have very distinct expectations for your work. They may differ on assignment instructions, project turn-around time, required writing styles or formats, supervision styles, feedback, or acceptable work management routines. Conflicting priorities or deadlines among their projects may be an issue. If each supervisor is reasonable in coordinating your work, your position will be less difficult.

Do you have your own support staff, or do you share support staff? Your support staff situation will greatly alter how you organize your time and work. Legal employers have drastically reduced support staff to save costs. Secretaries, paralegals, and legal assistants typically work for multiple lawyers. Firms often use either an in-house transcription pool or an outside transcription service. If you share staff time, realize that you will always need to schedule your requests for assistance around their prior obligations to other lawyers.

Does your firm work on a paperless or "less paper" basis? Some firms have become nearly 100 percent paperless, whereas other firms have achieved a "less paper" standard. Calendaring, timekeeping, billing, and document assembly have become electronic at most firms.

At many firms, client files have gone partially electronic but not completely so. The extent to which case management, document management, or practice management software has been adopted varies greatly among firms.

You will need to determine how the paperless or "less paper" operations at your firm will impact your time and work management strategies. With any increase in the amount of paper you must handle, you will need to be more systematic about your management of client files and documents. If your law firm has not developed sufficient systems for tracking the paperwork, then you will need to develop systems of your own.

What library resources and staff does your law firm have available? The time and work parameters for your research projects will vary substantially depending on your firm's resources and staffing. Your firm may limit use of electronic databases or not have access to the same ones you used previously. You may be directed to complete as much research as possible manually or with free Internet sources. If your firm has a limited library collection, you may need the local courthouse or law school libraries to supplement your firm's resources.

If librarians are on staff at your firm, they can potentially complete some initial research for you. When you are working on a project in an unfamiliar practice area or jurisdiction, they can save you time by recommending specific treatises, form books, and appropriate electronic resources. Law librarians can also suggest more efficient and effective research methods for your project.

Does your firm use document assembly software, template databases, or research databases? Many firms purchase software programs for document assembly if they are available for their jurisdictions or legal specialties. Other firms create their own template databases to streamline the drafting of frequently used documents. Most lawyers also create some personal templates for correspondence and special-purpose documents. Some firms have legal memoranda databases so that a lawyer saves time by just updating research previously completed. The sophistication of your firm in these areas will impact the time you spend on a work product.

How do your firm's billing mechanisms impact you? Whether your firm uses alternative fee arrangements, billable hours, or a non-billable basis will influence your decisions about time and work management. You will need to be clear about any limits on time, budgets for subscription electronic resources, or other billing variables before you begin a project.

For firms using billable hours, associates will input all their time on a project, and the supervising lawyer will discount the time and costs for the client's actual bill. Even firms with alternative fee arrangements may track lawyers' time to develop better historical data to set fees or to evaluate lawyers' efficiency. Legal employers on a non-billable basis may still have other measures in place such as number of matters completed or client satisfaction ratings.

What other policies does your firm have that impact your time and work management? Read your employee handbook carefully and listen up in training sessions and department meetings. Legal employers often have procedures and policies that are passed on verbally but never mentioned in written materials. Additionally, some items are known by everyone who worked at the firm when a decision was made but are never passed on to those who join the firm later. Be very careful that you do not make assumptions about best practices at the firm based on your law school experience or prior employment.

Are there legal trends for your firm's region, your specialty areas, or legal technology that you need to consider? Be aware that your law firm's priorities today may change. Economic exigencies alter an employer's perspective in many ways, including budget cuts in firm resources, level of staffing, growth practice areas, and concerns regarding client retention. Rapidly changing technology causes firms to consider new work methods: outsourcing low-level work, delivering services over the Internet, and marketing through social media.

If you are aware of the trends, you may be able to use your time and work management skills to prepare yourself for anticipated changes. You could spend time developing expertise in a growing practice area as work in your own specialty shrinks. You may take time to expand your technology skills so that you can offer expertise in new marketing or delivery methods.

Your legal environment greatly impacts your ability to do your work in a timely and effective manner. You can plan your own time and work management; however, if you do not take into account the characteristics of your environment, your best laid plans may fall apart. Note that the time and work management strategies in this book will travel well to new legal environments as you change employment. However, you will want to make adjustments based on the specifics of your new legal environment.

Reflection and Strategies

1. Which characteristics of your legal environment may make it easier for you to implement new time and work management strategies?
2. Which characteristics of your legal environment may make it harder for you to implement those changes?
3. Are there certain characteristics of your legal environment about which you need more information to assess their possible impact on implementing new strategies?

Basic Work Management Parameters

You need to organize your personal work environment to maximize your productivity. Your work organization creates a first impression for clients who enter your office and colleagues who will be working with you. You want the layout of your workspace to put everything within easy reach. You do not want to waste valuable minutes on a project looking for the items that you need. You want to choose equipment that makes you more efficient and effective in your work.

ORGANIZING YOUR PHYSICAL WORKSPACE
Decide what you need for office furniture. You may have been issued the same standard office furniture and equipment as every other lawyer in the building. However, if you do have an opportunity to request new or additional furniture, keep the following things in mind:

- Separate modular furniture components will give you the optimal variety to arrange your workspace for comfort and functionality. You can choose from a variety of modules:
  - straight desks, L-shaped desks, U-shaped desks
  - credenzas with shelves, file drawers, or pull-out printer storage
  - desk returns for left or right placement
  - lateral or vertical files with varying numbers of drawers, heights, and widths
  - hutch units with bookshelves, supply shelves, or storage units with doors
- Request furniture that fits your personal body measurements. Our shapes and sizes determine which office furniture is comfortable for us. Height, body shape, length of arms and legs—it matters what the furniture proportions are in relation to the individual.
- Request a really good chair. This statement does not mean mahogany and leather. It means ergonomically correct to fend off fatigue after long hours at your desk. Ask for a chair that provides upper-

back support and has adjustable arms, seat height, and lumbar support.

- If you will be meeting clients in your office, request a small round conference table with two to four chairs for a corner of your workspace. You and the client can move away from your desk to a more comfortable workspace without clutter.

- If a conference table will not fit into your space, consider asking for a desk that has a bow front or pull-out writing shelves on the side where your clients will sit. They will appreciate having a place to write or set a tablet while still having room when their chairs are pulled up to the desk.

- Choose a desk with the right combination of office supply drawers and filing drawers for your needs. If the desk does not have adequate storage, request a credenza, a hutch, or filing-cabinet units to supplement the desk storage.

- If your firm is paperless, your filing-cabinet needs will be minimal. If your firm merely uses "less paper," you will want to consider the amount of filing-cabinet space needed within your own office to supplement any central filing for the entire firm.

- Lateral file cabinets allow you to retrieve files easily from a seated position. Many of these units come with bookshelf or hutch arrangements above the lateral files. Lateral files will take up more floor space, however, than conventional vertical files.

- Consider mobile file-drawer towers, which can be wheeled under your credenza or desk for storage and later wheeled out for easy use at your conference table or next to your desk during a project. These are especially ideal for lawyers who reference their files regularly but need minimal file space.

- If you have your own printer instead of being connected to a network printer, think carefully about space. A printer on your desk surface will take more space than is desirable. Consider a credenza with a pull-out tray for your printer if you have enough space within your chair and desk arrangement for a printer tray to be extended.

Decide how you want to arrange your workspace. Even with a cookie-cutter selection of furniture, you will be able to design the flow of your workspace, unless everything is built-in. Here are some things to think about when arranging your furniture within your office space:

- Arrange your desk and computer work area so that either your back is to the door or the door is to one side and out of your peripheral vision when you are working. By positioning yourself so you are not directly looking into the hallway, you will be less distracted by traffic in the hall. People are more likely to stop and chat if they catch your eye as they walk by the door.
- Consider arranging your desk, computer work station, and credenza in a U-shape. You will be able to work at your desk and rotate your chair to your computer keyboard and additional work surfaces with ease.
- Have the open end of your U-shaped work area face the rest of your office space. You will be able to roll your desk chair out to the other work areas in the room: additional bookshelves, conference table, filing cabinets.
- Think about ergonomics when setting up your workspace. By having chair height, computer keyboard position, monitor height, and other aspects correctly measured, you will be able to work in comfort with fewer risks of back strain, eye strain, neck pain, and repetitive strain injury.

ORGANIZING YOUR WORK SURFACES

Keep your work areas organized so you can be more productive. For the lawyer in a paperless office who deals mainly with electronic files, it is easier to keep work areas fairly clear and neat. There are still many legal employers, however, who deal with large quantities of paper every day. In those environments, a lawyer needs to be proactive about managing the paper flow in his or her office.

We have all seen instances of colleagues' work surfaces so stacked with books and papers that there is no place to work on a project. Not

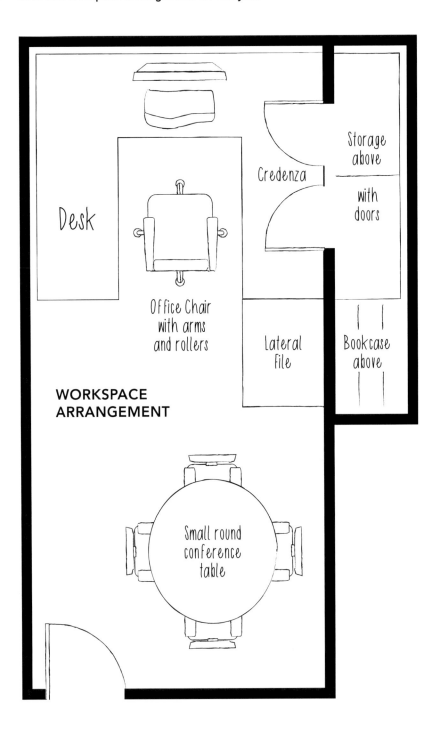

Desk

Office Chair
with arms
and rollers

Credenza

Storage
above

with
doors

Lateral
File

Bookcase
above

Small round
conference
table

**WORKSPACE
ARRANGEMENT**

only does the mess give an unappealing impression of the office occupant, it also means that time is wasted looking for items.

How neat your office needs to be will vary with your circumstances. If you meet with clients in your office, then you have less latitude. Some work on the desk will indicate a busy lawyer. However, precarious stacks of files and mounds of paper will make a client wonder if you will be organized enough to handle the case properly.

Another concern, of course, is confidentiality. If you have clients sitting on the opposite side of your desk, you do not want them to learn about someone else's legal problems because they can easily view file names and documents in the work spread out on your desk.

Your work surfaces will become temporarily messy while in the midst of several research or drafting projects—this is totally understandable. However, when a project is completed, remove the items that are no longer needed to make room for the next project. The books need to go back to the library, and the files need to go back into the file cabinet.

If you cannot find something on your desk within two to three minutes, you definitely need to minimize the piles that are hiding important papers. If you regularly get distracted because another stack of papers catches your eye and pulls you away from the important task in front of you, you also need to clear the piles.

Here are some tips for managing your work surfaces for greater productivity:

- Begin by clearing everything off of your desk and other work surfaces. The following points will suggest how you reallocate the space.
- Keep a large area in the center of your desk surface clear so you actually have room to work on a project. Preferably use this *all-clear zone* for working on only one task at a time.
- To the left of your all-clear zone, have one or more stacks of files and papers organized in order of priority for your work during the day. These are your *to-do stacks* of work that must be completed before you go home.

- In front of you, at the top of the all-clear zone, have other stacks for papers and files that you will use during the day.[1] These stacks may be arranged from left to right in whatever order you desire:
  - The *incoming stack* will include incoming mail, phone messages, reports, or other new items that arrive on your desk throughout the day. You will sort these items during the day and determine what to do with them. Chapter 4 will discuss how to deal with items in your incoming stack.
  - The *outgoing stack* will include items that you have completed during the day. A wide variety of items will go into this stack: letters ready to be mailed, work delegated to others in the firm, files to be returned to central file storage, books to go back to the firm's library. You may prefer to have multiple outgoing stacks sorted by item category.
  - The *refer-to stack* will include files and papers that you will need during the day for telephone calls, e-mail replies, or queries from staff. In other words, you may not be completing specific tasks on these items but expect to reference them at some point during the day.
  - The *meeting stack* will include files and papers that you need for client appointments or committee meetings during the day. These items also may not need additional work beforehand but will be ready at the time scheduled on your calendar.
- *Reference files* with information that you use regularly should go into a file drawer in your desk or credenza for easy access. These file folders might be sorted and labeled by court venue, committee, staff member name, professional association, practice area, restaurant menus, or any other suitable categories.
- Your small desk drawers should include all office supplies that you regularly need: pens, highlighters, paper clips, spring clips, rubber bands. Restock the drawers at least once a month rather than wait to run out of something.

---

1. Alternatively, you could have stacks on your credenza work surface if your desk area will not accommodate everything.

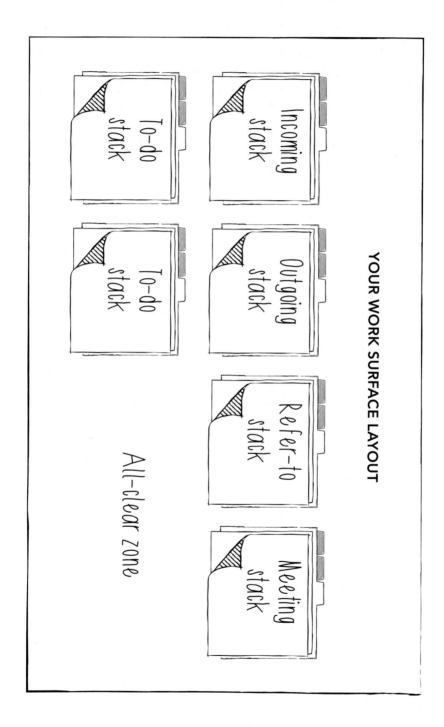

YOUR WORK SURFACE LAYOUT

- The top of your desk should have only tools and equipment that you use regularly: telephone, pen/pencil holder, stapler, tape dispenser, staple remover, paper clip holder. If you do not use an item regularly, put it in a drawer instead or on the credenza.
- Your desk left- or right-return work surface should include only your computer essentials: laptop or desktop CPU, screen, keyboard, and mouse. A printer can go here or on a credenza pull-out tray.
- Ideally your credenza work surface should also have only items that you use regularly:
  - your hard-copy appointment calendar or daily planner
  - a tray for computer paper for your printer
  - a stack of reading material: articles, journals, newsletters
  - books used regularly
- Other items that were previously on your work surfaces should now be sorted:
  - Paperwork for future tasks (as opposed to current tasks) should be organized within a desk or credenza file drawer using the *tickler file* system discussed in Chapter 4.
  - Other important items should be refiled in filing cabinets, returned to bookshelves, or placed in other office storage spaces.
  - Anything that was unearthed that is no longer needed should be thrown away or shredded.

Straighten up your work areas several times a day as needed. Before you go to lunch, take a few minutes to put away things that you are finished with and police the area for stray papers, notes, paper clips, pens, and other items. When you have a spare couple of minutes during the day, straighten up your work surfaces before moving on to the next task. At night, take a few minutes to straighten up your work area. Put away things that you no longer need.

Before you go home each evening, determine what papers and files will go in your to-do and refer-to stacks for the next day. Any items left in your outgoing stack should be distributed to the appropriate locations. If anything has remained in your incoming stack, it needs to be sorted and dealt with before leaving for the day using the system discussed in Chapter 4.

ORGANIZING AND MANAGING CLIENT FILES

Law firms differ on the paperless and "less paper" dichotomy. Some firms have successfully switched to paperless client files. In this system, every piece of paper is immediately scanned into searchable PDF format upon arrival at the firm; correspondence is handled electronically; and all client files are electronically available through case management, document management, or practice management software. The cost-savings and security benefits of paperless files have been touted for a number of years. Lost files are a thing of the past. Multiple lawyers can access an electronic file simultaneously.

If you are in a paperless environment, keep the following steps in mind to ensure that you are most productive and not creating obstacles in an otherwise successful paperless system:

- Attend any lawyer training that your firm offers on its chosen case management, document management, or practice management technology. When later upgrades occur, determine whether you need additional training.
- Have client papers scanned immediately upon arrival so that the electronic client file is updated and papers are not lost inadvertently before scanning.
- Use the correct file-naming conventions when you scan documents so everyone can find them easily.

Many firms have gone the "less paper" route rather than the paperless one and still work with some hard-copy files that have to be managed. These firms may not have the technology, staff, or money to transition fully to paperless files. Or they may have a client base that is not paperless and expects all matters to be handled with hard-copy documents. In some locales, local courts also may not be paperless.

If your office is paperless, the remainder of this section on organizing and managing client files will not pertain to you; you can skip to the next main topic in this chapter. For our purposes in the remainder of this section, we will assume that you are working in a firm that has not achieved paperless status. When you are handling hard-copy client files, you do not want to be the person responsible for a missing document or file. Therefore, make sure that you fully understand your firm's systems for accessing or storing files and for tracking file actions and deadlines.

An individual lawyer may be solely responsible for many clients, and some of those clients may have multiple matters. Follow these steps to stay updated on each legal matter without having client files stacked on every surface:

- Keep only the files that you plan to deal with during the current day on your work surfaces: files on which you have tasks to complete, you know you will need for reference, or you will need for appointments or meetings. Place these files in your to-do, refer-to, or meeting stacks as described earlier in this chapter.
- Client files you use regularly for current matters should be in your immediate work area file storage: desk file drawer, mobile file-drawer tower, or filing cabinet. After a matter has been concluded or no longer needs attention in the near future, the file should go back into the main file storage for your office.
- If you have a large number of files that you use regularly for current matters, you may not have enough filing-cabinet space in your own office. Stacked files on every available surface are unsightly and more likely to slide or get knocked to the floor—increasing the chance of documents being lost or misfiled.
- For extra storage space, consider using banker's boxes or heavy plastic storage boxes instead of just stacking files everywhere. The boxes can be open or lidded depending on the file size. Lidded boxes can be neatly stacked to one side if necessary. Open boxes can be arranged on the floor underneath or near your desk.
- If you choose boxes that come in a variety of bright colors, you can personalize a sorting system by using different colored boxes

for different types of files. Design a system that matches your clients and tasks:

- priority of the work (red for *urgent*, orange for *important*, blue for *by end of the week*)
- your multiple practice areas (red for *bankruptcy*, orange for *employment*, blue for *contract*)
- types of work (red for *research*, orange for *document drafting*, blue for *waiting for more information*)
- court dates (red for *this week*, orange for *next week*, blue for *later dates*)
- clients (red for *Patterson*, orange for *Chancellor*, blue for *Reed*)

DOCUMENT ASSEMBLY OR TEMPLATES TO ASSIST YOU IN YOUR WORK

Using document assembly software or other templates will save you a great deal of time in drafting documents—and it will save your clients money. Most firms will purchase subscription document assembly software if it is available for their jurisdictions and practice areas. Packages are readily available for states with a large number of lawyers and for several federal practice areas. Fortunately, some smaller companies are now producing software packages for additional states and legal specialty areas.

If your firm does not have access to subscription services because of jurisdiction, practice area, or cost, it has likely developed its own word-processing templates for the most frequently used documents in each practice area. Whenever possible, use document assembly or templates rather than reinventing the wheel. You will likely develop some additional templates for specialty documents that are unique to your own practice circumstances.

DICTATION VERSUS WORD PROCESSING VERSUS SPEECH RECOGNITION

Until the1990s, lawyers traditionally dictated their letters and legal documents and depended on secretaries or typing pools for the finished product. After word processing became commonplace, law firms reduced secretarial staff as more lawyers with word-processing skills were hired.

Although sources differ as to the exact figures, it is commonly argued that a lawyer using dictation can complete work three to five times faster than a lawyer using word processing. Such claims are often made by comparing dictation with word processing for set paragraphs, which is obviously not the natural work situation of a lawyer drafting letters or documents.

For many lawyers who have always word processed, dictation is awkward and takes practice before it becomes smooth and fast. Transcription errors may occur until the lawyer remembers to say "indented list" or "semicolon," to spell unusual words, and to stop the recorder while thinking. Making corrections during dictation also takes some practice.

It makes sense, however, that lawyers would dictate faster than they can type after the initial adjustment period. Most lawyers are self-taught typists with minimal speed and accuracy in their word processing. They are rarely professionally trained on nuances with Word or WordPerfect software. With the frequency of upgrades to software, lawyers find it frustrating to learn the differences between versions.

Compact digital voice recorders have made it convenient for lawyers to dictate anywhere. You can use your digital voice recorder for short reminders, documents, notes to files, instructions to your support staff, and much more. For lawyers who travel frequently, these compact recorders are excellent tools.

When choosing a digital voice recorder, consider these features to maximize convenience and flexibility:

- hours of recording
- battery life
- USB mass storage
- USB battery charging
- direct link to a PC or Mac
- MP3 plus 16-bit or WMA stereo recording
- microphone and headphone jacks

- index marks or track marks
- fast and slow playback speeds
- ability to correct in playback
- size of the LCD font
- tapeless format

For some lawyers, being able to see the words on the screen as they compose is more conducive to their working style than just hearing themselves dictate. With speech recognition software, your document appears on the screen while you speak. If you are a slow and inaccurate typist on your best days, speech recognition software may be especially beneficial.

Compared with older versions, it takes little time now to train the software to become attuned to your voice. If you have little experience with dictation, you will still need practice, however, before you can compose a perfect document or letter on the first draft.

A number of speech recognition products are on the market. One of the best-known legal products is Dragon NaturallySpeaking. The following list describes some of the features touted by the product's website:

- dictation in Word and compatibility with Excel and Outlook
- spoken commands to perform a wide variety of tasks, including correcting errors, e-mailing contacts, and changing format
- preloaded legal dictionaries with the flexibility to add practice area terms, client information, or other terms
- Bluetooth headset and digital voice recorder compatibility
- software for multiple-lawyer networks
- security enhancements

Your time and work management will be greatly enhanced if you organize your workspace, work surfaces, and client files. Document assembly and templates can greatly reduce drafting time. By intentionally choosing technology to improve your drafting capabilities, you will save time and increase your productivity.

....

Reflection and Strategies

1. Which additional furniture components would make your workspace more functional?
2. Which changes in the physical layout of your workspace would promote greater productivity or better workstation ergonomics?
3. What first impression about your abilities as a lawyer would a client have from looking at your work surfaces: disorganized because of the mess, efficient because of the clear desk and neatness, busy but organized because of the orderliness of the visible work?
4. If your work surfaces are cluttered or you have trouble finding important papers or files, what organizational issues need to be addressed to minimize the problems?
5. What organizational steps do you need to implement to avoid disorganized client files, misplaced documents, or lost client files?
6. What forms do you need to develop to be more efficient in your standard administrative tasks?
7. What templates do you need to develop to be more efficient in your standard correspondence tasks?
8. What additional document templates do you need to develop to be more efficient in your drafting tasks that are not covered by document assembly software?
9. Consider whether you would increase your productivity by using dictation or voice recognition software rather than depending solely on word processing.
10. List any additional training that you need in order to be more productive: word processing, document assembly software, case management software, other office equipment.

....

Basic Time Management Parameters

We all talk about needing more time: "If only I had more hours in the day." "If only I could find the time to do X." "If only I could find a way to save time." "If I just had more time, I could . . ."

Every week has 168 hours, or 10,080 minutes. Not a minute more or a minute less. Everyone has the same amount of time to accomplish important goals and live a satisfying life. You cannot have more. Realize that you cannot save time by wishing. You cannot find time by hoping. You must make time within your day, week, month, and year to accomplish what you want to do.

Lawyers could work 24 hours a day, 7 days a week, for 365 days and still have more to do. Work could easily consume all your time for the remainder of your life if you let it. You could always read another case, attend another CLE, write another draft, make another telephone call, send another e-mail, and log another billable unit.

However, do you really want to spend more time at the office? No! Instead you want to complete your projects, do a professional job for your clients, and still have time left over for your family, friends, and hobbies. You want to control your time rather than feel overwhelmed by conflicting demands, interruptions, lost time, and wasted time. To regain your sanity, you need to implement basic time management techniques and accomplish your work efficiently and effectively each day.

SETTING A ROUTINE WITHIN THE CHAOS

Many lawyers feel they have no control over their days. Everyone makes demands on their time without their having a say in the process. Senior lawyers assign new projects to complete. Colleagues stop by for impromptu discussions on their own projects. Telephone calls from clients with crises come at the most inopportune times. Meetings are called on short notice. Time is spent waiting at court. E-mails pour in by the hundreds. Five o'clock arrives with the morning's first project still sitting incomplete on the desk. Another late evening will be needed to complete the day's planned work.

It is necessary to take back control of your time. How easily you will be able to do so will depend on your will power, boundary setting, and persistence. It is up to you to navigate the chaos and enforce some routine within it. No one is going to do it for you. You need to choose strategies from this book that will allow you to become more productive in your work situation.

Evaluate your legal environment. In Chapter 2, you were asked a series of questions regarding your legal environment. Each of those answers will impact how you control your time and implement strategies.

You can gain more control and become more productive no matter how many practice areas you have, how many files you run, how many meetings you attend, and how many interruptions currently plague your work. You can moderate the number of late nights and weekends in the office. You need to choose strategies from this book that will allow you to become more productive in your specific work situation.

Understand the importance of efficiency and effectiveness. Efficiency is all about using time wisely. It is about expending only as much time as absolutely necessary on any task, finding faster ways to work, fitting the right-sized projects into the time available, and not wasting time. Effectiveness is about getting the maximum results out of your time, accomplishing the most important tasks in your day, and not allowing less important tasks to dominate your time.

By completing tasks each day in the most efficient and effective ways, you will be able to accomplish more for yourself, your clients, and your law firm. You will allot your time more wisely and choose strategies that produce greater results—working smarter rather than harder.

Understand the difference between a real crisis that you must handle and a "crisis" that you may not need to handle. A real *crisis* is something that demands your attention right now. A *most important* task is something that is related to a professional goal you want to accomplish. An *important* task still relates to a professional goal but is not as high priority. A *least important* task is one that has positive attributes but may not ultimately have high enough priority to be completed; its achievement is desirable rather than necessary.

First let's talk about the *ideal* day for a lawyer. We try to avoid our own tasks turning into crises by managing our time and completing our work well within any deadlines. We do so by completing as many of the most important tasks as possible each day. We move on to the important tasks after we have progressed as far as possible on the most important tasks of the day. Least important tasks round out our day if enough time is left, but these tasks can be moved to the next day if necessary.

Now let's talk about the *reality* of a lawyer's day. Real crises do occur because we deal with clients whose lives and legal circumstances have a certain amount of unpredictability. Depending on your practice area, you may be confronted by more legal crises than colleagues in other specialties. If you need to handle a crisis, you obviously do so immediately and return to your other tasks after the crisis is resolved.

No matter how well you monitor and complete your own tasks, other people will place demands on your time throughout the day: partners, colleagues, support staff. Sometimes these people will want you to pay immediate attention to a new task even though the task is not really a crisis and, in fact, may not even be very important. Your tendency may be to replace the most important or important task on which you are working with the task that seems to be a crisis to someone else.

Before you ignore the tasks on your desk and agree to switch to the requested task, evaluate that requested task carefully. Do not automatically accept that it is a real crisis and needs immediate attention. If you constantly give in to other persons' perceived (but not actual) crises, you will be the individual interrupted while other colleagues will have said no or "not now" in diplomatic ways.

Assuming that you determine the request is not a real crisis and can be delayed, you want to explain your work priorities and indicate that you will complete the task later within your workload or that someone else will need to complete the task if it is required sooner. An exception, of course, will be if the request is from the managing partner; in that case, you will probably acquiesce graciously if you think a discussion about priorities is not possible.

Realize that interruptions will occur, crises will arise, and some-one senior will make demands that you cannot refuse. You want to manage and control your time each day as much as possible. However, the reality is that life happens. The secret to dealing with interruptions, crises, and demands is to take them in stride. They may ruin your planned time management, but they do not have to ruin your day. When the unexpected happens, take a few minutes to decide the most efficient and effective way to deal with the matter.

Do not let these occurrences raise your blood pressure, leave you seething, or create unnecessary stress. Once the matter is dealt with, take a few minutes to regroup and then rework your schedule to get back on task.

Embrace time management as an ally rather than a ball and chain. Some lawyers worry that setting priorities, scheduling tasks, writing to-do lists, and using other techniques will take away all flexibility. They fear losing control rather than gaining it. To facilitate change, implement new strategies in stages rather than everything at once. You will be more successful with your initial strategies and more inclined to add new strategies in later weeks if you do not overwhelm yourself.

After adopting new techniques, stick with them over time. Do not expect instant results. Many lawyers reap the benefits of implementing new time management techniques within two or three weeks. They are more productive each day, feel less pressured in their work, and notice an improved quality in their work products. They often ask, "Why did I wait so long to do this?"

SETTING PROFESSIONAL GOALS AND PRIORITIES

By clarifying your goals and priorities, you will focus your efforts on the most important tasks rather than be distracted by tasks deserving less attention. You will be able to clearly evaluate each task on your desk. Goals state what you want to achieve; priorities organize the order of tasks to achieve those goals.

Choose goals for the coming year. You may have set goals as part of the yearly performance appraisal process at your firm. However, if you do not already have delineated goals, now is the perfect time to clarify the most important things for you to accomplish.

When thinking about your goals, keep your list realistic and manageable. If you limit your list to ten goals or less, you are more likely to organize your life around them. Setting unrealistic goals that you cannot attain or setting too many goals may cause you to become discouraged and abandon your efforts.

Also, write goals that are specific and measurable. Specific goals are more achievable because they avoid vagueness as to what you want to accomplish. Make each of your goals measurable so that you will know when the goal has been met. For each goal, have one or more objective measures against which you can assess your progress.

If you are new to implementing goals, you may be more comfortable choosing a smaller number of goals and limiting the time period for your goals to three or six months rather than an entire one-year period. Here are some thoughts on which professional goals to choose:

- Select goals that will make you more valuable to your employer (examples: increase your expertise in your practice area, become more proficient in electronic research).
- Select goals that will make you more efficient in your job (examples: set aside uninterrupted project time each day, decrease e-mail interruptions).
- Select goals that will make you more effective in your job (examples: work on projects during the day in priority order, delegate tasks when appropriate).

For each goal, list multiple strategies you can undertake to help you achieve the goal. Under each strategy, list tasks you can complete to implement the strategy. For example, if your goal is to gain greater expertise in your practice area, one strategy might be to find out about continuing legal education seminars, and a second strategy might be to find out about publications in your field that you could read. Each strategy would list specific tasks to help you implement the strategy. You would also list the measurements that you will use to determine whether you have achieved the goal. See the example of the strategies, tasks, and measures exercise for goals.

● ●

Strategies, Tasks, and Measures for a Professional Goal

GOAL: Increase my expertise in my practice area.

STRATEGY 1: Find out what courses are being provided by approved CLE sources.

TASKS:
1. Check the online catalogs for current CLE offerings from at least two providers.
2. Sign up for e-mail announcements on new offerings from those providers.
3. Check the local and state bar websites for additional CLE offerings.

STRATEGY 2: Learn about books, journals, and other materials in my practice area.

TASKS:
1. Talk to the firm librarians about new resources and firm subscriptions.
2. Visit the ABA publications website to search for new titles.
3. Read the book reviews in legal journals/newspapers in my practice area.
4. Talk with other lawyers about what they are reading in our practice area.

MEASURES (by the end of the year):
1. Attend two CLE seminars.
2. Read one book recently published in my practice area.
3. Get on the routing list for any firm subscriptions for journals/newsletters in my practice area.
4. Schedule reading time every two weeks.

Revisit your goals list each month to evaluate your progress. If appropriate, you may want to consider new strategies for reaching your goals. Also consider new tasks for each strategy that will help you meet your goals more easily. Modify your measures as needed if you enter new strategies or tasks. If a goal has been met completely, determine whether you are ready to add a new goal to your list. If so, complete the same strategies, tasks, and measures steps for that new goal.

Start an ongoing master list of future tasks you need to complete. The first tasks to go on your *master list* will be those generated in the above goals-strategies-tasks exercise. You will then add tasks that relate to your work generally. Regular tasks that you complete weekly, monthly, or annually should go on the list. Examples of these regular tasks might be weekly review of client invoices, monthly status reports for a committee you chair, or quarterly file reviews. You will also add new tasks that arrive daily in your mail sort, are assigned by partners, or are related to a new project.

Do not assume that you will remember all the things that you need to finish over the next several months or year. Without a written reminder, you may overlook an item—even one that you have previously completed on a regular basis. Items on your master list will be scheduled later for action at the appropriate time. You will consult your master list to determine your priorities for the next month.

Choose task priorities for the month.[1] Right before the beginning of the month, compose your task priority list for that month. Any current projects that will continue into the month should be added to the list. Select from your master list any tasks with due dates during the month. Some of those tasks may relate to administrative requirements by your firm, such as a quarterly review of client files or required reports. Consider your goals and the related strategies and tasks; include several of those tasks on your monthly list. Finally, include time and work management techniques you plan to implement to increase your productivity.

---

1. Although the sample lists in this chapter are typed versions, you could use task-list software as well for all the task priority lists (master, monthly, weekly, and daily). If you feel overwhelmed by having four categories of lists, begin with weekly and daily lists.

During the month, as you sort your daily incoming mail, e-mails, and telephone messages, you will add tasks to the appropriate list—the master list for longer-range future tasks or the monthly list for tasks to be completed during the current month. If actual deadlines are known, add those deadlines to your calendar as well as to the list.

Next to items with deadlines on your monthly list, note the date on which you tentatively plan to begin the task. By reviewing your monthly list regularly, you will be able to see what project deadlines are approaching and what lead time you need for their completion. A sample monthly task list is provided to illustrate these steps.

By making a list of your task priorities for the month, you are more likely to accomplish all of them. You will be more comfortable if you have everything captured and will not inadvertently forget something that you meant to do.

Choose task priorities for the coming week. Determine what you need to accomplish in the next workweek. Move items from your monthly list to your weekly list as appropriate. Ask yourself whether there are any additional items to address that have come to your attention but were not included on your master or monthly lists. Indicate next to each item any deadline associated with it.

Prioritize your tasks for the week. Divide the list into the three main categories mentioned earlier in this chapter:[2]

- *most important* tasks (relate to professional goals you want to achieve)
- *important* tasks (relate to professional goals but are not as high priority)
- *least important* tasks (have positive attributes but may not ultimately have high enough priority to be completed; achievement is desirable rather than necessary).

---

2. See the discussion on pages 24–25 in this chapter regarding real crises and perceived crises. Remember that a real crisis will be given precedence over the most important tasks on your list.

Within each category, prioritize the tasks if more than one is listed. Your priority may be indicated by numbers (1, 2, 3, and so forth) or letters (A, B, C, and so forth). If you prioritize within a category as you write the list, the tasks will be written down in their priority order.

• •

January Task List

○ Anderson project: **deadline 1/31, begin 1/15**
   a. Talk to firm librarian re: interlibrary loan of Smith treatise
   b. Update research since September
   c. Draft client letter on update and next steps

○ Complete monthly status report for marketing subcommittee on social media: **deadline 1/20, begin 1/18**

○ Reynolds file: letter to client regarding completed research

○ Johnson file: check on expert witness report

○ Collins file: discuss settlement strategies with client

○ Write article for the firm website about recent Court of Appeals opinions

○ **1/18** Attend CLE regarding ethics and file CLE reporting form with bar

○ Review client invoices for billable units and descriptions: **deadline each Friday, begin each Tuesday.**

○ Discuss new tickler file system with Jenn and Max

○ Ask IT to help set up archive file folders for e-mail

○ **1/21** Attend John Quinn-Jones retirement dinner (remembrance stories due to HR by **1/9**)

[You would add to this list as new developments occur throughout the month.]

Alternatively, you can prioritize after you have written the entire list for a category.

For the most important tasks, estimate how long each task will take. Keeping your priority in mind for each task, indicate the day or days when you tentatively plan to focus on it. Complete the same estimating and scheduling steps for the important tasks. For the least important tasks, leave the days open and determine during the week when you will work on those tasks. A sample weekly task priorities list is provided to illustrate these steps.

It is best to complete your list for the coming week on your last workday before you leave for the weekend. You will then be able to start immediately on the most important tasks when your new work-week begins. You are more likely to relax during your weekend because you will know that you are organized for the coming week.

Choose task priorities for the next day each evening before you leave work. During the week, you will include additional tasks on your master, monthly, and weekly lists as new developments occur in the office. Refer to your weekly list to determine which tasks should now be moved to your daily list. Be realistic about how many tasks you will be able to complete given your scheduled client appointments, meetings, and other obligations.

Although you already tentatively prioritized and scheduled the first two categories of tasks (most important and important) for your week, you need to reevaluate those decisions in light of any changed circumstances: new tasks that have been assigned to you, delays in completing a task as planned, changes in deadlines. Once you have reevaluated the previous priorities on your weekly list, move tasks to your list for the next day and determine the priorities within each of the first two task categories. Finally, consider your least important tasks for the week and whether any of those tasks should be included for the next day.

By completing your list before you leave in the evening, you will feel more positive about your upcoming workday because you will be mentally prepared for it. A sample daily task list is provided to illustrate these steps.

• •

Task List for the Week of January 6

MOST IMPORTANT

#1 Johnson file: check expert witness report; **MON**
#2 Collins file: discuss settlement strategies with client; **MON**
#3 Finish remembrance story for HR for Quinn-Jones **1/9 deadline; TUES**
#4 Review A–G client invoices **1/10 deadline; TUES & WED**
#5 Clarify tickler file procedure with Jenn and discuss problems; **WED**

IMPORTANT

#1 Review Court of Appeals opinions for article; **MON**
#2 Begin article draft for the website; **TUES**
#3 Finish article draft for the website; **THURS**
#4 Talk to print center regarding binding error last week; **THURS**
#5 Edit article draft and send it to Max; **FRI**

LEAST IMPORTANT

Ask Jenn about status of binder order for next month's meeting

[The items in the Most Important and Important categories were written in priority order (indicated with bold number) as the list was composed. Alternatively, a list for each category could be written and the priorities decided and indicated after the full list was formulated. You would add to the list and reprioritize as new developments occur during the week.]

Consult your daily task list four times during the day. You will consult your daily task list when you first arrive in the morning. As you become more adept at formulating your daily task lists and increasing your daily productivity, you will find that your initial priorities for the

● ●

Tasks for Tuesday, January 7

MOST IMPORTANT

#1 Finish remembrance story for HR for Quinn-Jones
    deadline 1/9
#2 Review A–G client invoices **today and WED**
#3 Respond to letter for Acton file
#4 Check with Molly re: initial research for Peterson
    phone query
#5 Discuss Smithson file with Dan

IMPORTANT

#1 Begin article draft for the website
#2 Sign group card for Joe's wedding before 4:00 p.m.

LEAST IMPORTANT

Ask Jenn about binder status

[Note that several new tasks developed on Monday that
would have been added to the weekly task list and then
designated for today's task list. You will add new tasks and
reprioritize throughout the day as needed.]

day will stay unchanged most days. However, the reality is that you may
have to reprioritize during the day because of unexpected events. Plan
to review your list and priorities three additional times during your day:
mid-morning, lunch time, and mid-afternoon. Make any adjustments
required because of new tasks that may have arrived on your desk or
other circumstances.

**Should personal tasks and professional tasks be on the same
list?** We all have personal errands to complete: get the car inspected,
make a dinner reservation, purchase birthday presents, telephone for
a dental appointment. Some lawyers prefer to have a separate list for
these items. Others want to include these reminders on their daily work-

related task list so that all tasks are in one place. If colleagues will have access to your task list, you will probably want separate lists for professional and personal items. Otherwise, it is purely personal preference how you track these additional tasks.

ORGANIZING YOUR DEADLINES AND IMPORTANT DATES

Lawyers are constantly faced with deadlines, appointments, meetings, and court dates. The consequences of missing a statute of limitations, a docket call, or a meeting with a major client are obvious. Many firms depend on electronic calendaring software that includes e-mail and contact capabilities. Some firms are using sophisticated case management or practice management software that integrates the calendaring function with other management functions, including time capture, billing, and document management. With the variety of available applications (apps), you can also have your office calendar accessible on your smartphone if synchronization with your firm's software is possible.

If you frequently work on large projects with multiple stages and deadlines, you may want to consider project management software.[3] Alternatively, you can use a dry-erase, month-at-a-glance wall calendar to track the project stages. If your projects tend to be completed over several months, get a multiple-month or year-long version.

Beware of relying solely on electronic calendars. Disruption will result when the computer system crashes and you cannot access your appointments, court dates, and meetings. Even if the disruption lasts for only a short time, it will be difficult to manage your calendar until the technology is back online. The circumspect lawyer will always have an individual back-up system as well as any calendar provided by the firm. By having calendars in multiple formats, you will be certain that important dates are captured and accessible.

The old-fashioned hard-copy daily planner or appointments calendar is a good option for a backup. Every time a court date or statute of

---

3. Project management software can be used to produce color-coded Gantt charts, which allow you to visualize the stages of a project and the overlap of tasks. Gantt charts clearly delineate starting dates, deadlines, and responsibilities for the separate stages.

limitations is entered into the firm's centralized system for one of your client files, it should also be entered on the hard-copy calendar. Every time you enter a deadline or event on your individual electronic calendar, also enter it on the hard-copy version. If you and your assigned staff member both update the firm's centralized system as well as your individual electronic calendar, then both of you must update the hard-copy version as well.

However, you have to *look at* the calendar regularly for it to help you. People elaborately enter appointments into their smartphones, tablets, or daily planners and then later miss the very same appointments because they never looked at the calendar. Pre-set reminders for electronic calendars are useful, but only if the lawyer is aware of the computer or smartphone alert when it occurs.

ORGANIZING INCOMING AND OUTGOING ITEMS[4]
If you are fortunate, you will have a staff member who opens your mail, sorts it along with any new internal items, and prioritizes everything in the incoming stack before you even see any of the items on your desk. However, if that is not the case, you need to establish a system to handle the items that land in your incoming stack throughout the day.

You will be less likely to overlook an urgent request if you sort your incoming stack three times a day on a regular schedule: once in the morning, once midday, and again before going home in the evening. You want to make decisions as to the status of each incoming item as quickly as possible when sorting. Avoid just returning the item to your stack because you are unsure what to do with it.

You have probably heard of the OHIO method: Only Handle It Once. Some items can be handled once and taken care of immediately. In reality, however, many items will need later attention and will be added to your task lists (master, monthly, weekly, or daily) for action at the appropriate time.

---

4. In Chapter 3, pages 12 and 15 discuss an organizational system for your desk: incoming and outgoing stacks; stacks categorized as items to do, items to refer to, and items for meetings; and reference files in your desk drawer. If you need more information on these systems, please refer to those pages.

For each item in your incoming stack, make one of the following decisions:

- **File it.**
  - **Client Item:** Items pertinent to client matters that do not need action. In a paperless office, follow the procedures for scanning the item to the client file. In other offices, note the client file-matter designation for the staff member who will do the filing and then place the item in your outgoing stack.
  - **Reference Item:** Items not relating to client matters that you want to keep handy for future reference, such as a directory for your local bar association, flyer with holiday closings for the area courts, newsletter from a community agency, or local symphony concert schedule.
    - Ask yourself whether you really need to keep the item. Does someone else in the firm retain the information? Is the information online?
    - Are you likely to use the item? If you are uncertain, place a date at the top of the item to indicate when you will discard it if you have not used the information.
    - File these items in your file drawer in the reference file folders you previously labeled by category.
    - If the reference item is updated periodically, consider whether the last edition can now be discarded when you file the new edition.
    - Each time you go to a reference file folder, discard any items that you have not used by the date noted for potential discard.
    - Clean out these files at least twice a year. Discard items that are no longer relevant.
- **Forward it.** If the information is relevant to someone else in your firm but not to you, attach a preprinted routing slip with the person's name and any additional message. Then place the item in your outgoing stack for distribution. See a sample of the routing slip below.

TO:

FROM: [Your name preprinted]

I thought the attached item might be of interest to you.
Discard it or retain it as you see fit.

[Add any other comments here.]

- **Do it.** If completing the task related to the item will take less than fifteen minutes, take care of it immediately if you have the time available. Then place the completed item in your outgoing stack for distribution or filing as appropriate.
- **Delegate it.** If someone else can handle the task for you without a face-to-face discussion before delegation, attach a preprinted delegation form[5] with the person's name and any instructions. Then place the item in your outgoing stack for distribution. See a sample of the delegation form below.

TO:

FROM: [Your name preprinted]

Please complete the following tasks for me regarding the attached information. If you have any questions, please let me know. Thank you.

[Add any instructions here, including any deadline date.]

---

5. Chapter 6 will discuss delegation in detail.

- **Schedule it.** Add the item to your task lists as appropriate (master, monthly, weekly, or daily) and prioritize the task within the list if necessary. Calendar any related deadlines to the item.
  - The paperwork can be temporarily filed in your tickler file if it is scheduled beyond your current day's list of tasks (see the next section on setting up a tickler file).
  - If the item will be completed the same day, add it to the to-do stack on your desk in a position within the stack in relation to its priority.
- **Read it.** Only keep items that you will read. Do not put newsletters, catalogs, journals, and other items in this stack if you know you will just throw them out later, still unread.
  - If the item is routed to you and others in the firm, request that your name be placed last on the routing list so the item will automatically come to you as the final reader. You will then be able to keep it until you have read it without preventing others on the routing slip from seeing it.
  - If it is not possible to be last on the routing slip, send the item on to another person on the list without checking off your name. Repeat this step until it returns and you are the only person who has not read it.
  - If the magazine or newsletter is your personal subscription or mail and does not need to be kept permanently, quickly look at the table of contents and decide whether there is anything you need to read. If not, throw the magazine or newsletter away. If you are interested in just one or two articles, rip out the relevant items and throw the rest of the issue away. Alternatively, note the page numbers for relevant articles on the front cover so you can quickly flip to them later.
  - If the routed item or subscription is no longer of interest to you, ask to have your name removed from the routing slip or cancel the subscription.
  - Place your reading stack on your desk or credenza where it is in reach but not in the way. Schedule reading time on your calendar at least once every two weeks.

- If your reading stack gets higher than four inches, it is time to cull it. Spend a few minutes at the end of a day and throw out any items that are now out of date or no longer of interest.
- **Trash it.** Do not keep anything that does not fall into one of the categories above.

SUPPLEMENT YOUR INCOMING SORT PROCESS WITH A TICKLER FILE

A *tickler file* is a series of file folders that helps you organize items that you will need for future tasks on your lists (master, monthly, weekly, or daily) or future events. By using a tickler file, you avoid having your work surface covered with multiple stacks of documents that are not currently needed. You will also be less likely to misplace an important paper.

In a desk or credenza file drawer, set up twelve file folders or hanging files labeled for the months of the year. The front file folder will be for the current month. Behind the current month's file folder, place additional file folders or hanging files labeled for the individual dates within the month (use the appropriate number of date file folders for the current month: 31, 30, 29, or 28). Place the other months' file folders behind the current month and its date files; these later months will not have date file folders.

- For example, if the current month is May, you will have May as the first file folder, followed by file folders in numerical order 1–31. The file folders for the months of June through April would then follow the last date file folder (31) for May.
- In each monthly file folder, have a sheet of paper on which you have listed all the tasks that are completed during that month on a regular basis: a monthly report, monthly review of client files, preparation for a monthly committee meeting, quarterly file review completed in that month. This list of standard tasks that occur each year during that month will prevent you from accidentally forgetting any recurring task.

TICKLER FILE SYSTEM

- Behind the list in each monthly file folder, place correspondence, notes, forms, or other papers that relate to any tasks for that month. Everything related to the tasks for the month will now be available at the appropriate time. Remember to add the tasks to the appropriate task list as well (master, monthly).
- When you come to the current month, in this case May, you will sort the materials in the monthly file folder and redistribute them among the date file folders (1–31) to match completion of the tasks during the month in coordination with your task lists (monthly, weekly, daily) and calendar deadlines. You will check your date folder each evening for the items contained in it for the next day's tasks.
- You can use your tickler file system for items that pertain to events on future dates as well as for tasks. You can file the announcement for a future lecture or symposium at the local law school. You can place season tickets for various concerts, plays, or sporting events in envelopes at the appropriate months or dates.

THE SMALL, MISCELLANEOUS TASKS NOT ON YOUR TASK LISTS

All lawyers are inundated with small, miscellaneous tasks that do not warrant a place on task lists. The reminders accumulate on random slips of paper, sticky notes, and message slips that can get lost on your desk. It is easy to become immune to these types of notes over a series of days and no longer even register their existence.

With Microsoft Outlook or other software, you can categorize electronic task lists and label one of them *Miscellaneous* for these tasks. You will be able to track completed tasks if you choose that view of the list. Alternatively, you may want to add these tasks to your computer desktop on electronic sticky notes.

However, several disadvantages occur with any electronic methods. You will not have access if there is a disruption in your computer service. In addition, the extra mouse clicks and keystrokes may be a nuisance if you are in the middle of a project when a new task comes to your attention. With electronic sticky notes, your desktop screen can become very cluttered by the end of the week with these reminders.

Using an old-fashioned stenographer's (steno) spiral pad is one of the easiest ways to capture small requests, phone numbers for returning calls, or reminders. Keep the pad within reach on your work surface at all times. When someone calls and asks you to undertake a miscellaneous task, write it on the steno pad. When someone stops by your office and asks you to do something minor, write it on the steno pad. When you have a random thought about something you need to consider later or are concerned you will forget, add it to the steno pad.

For each new item that goes on your steno pad, put the current date, write a brief description of the task, include a due date if desired, leave an extra inch for later notes, and then draw a line under it. If the task is critical or needs to be done quickly, use a symbol (exclamation point, star) or colored highlighter to indicate the importance.

When you attempt to telephone the person related to the task and leave a voicemail message, write the date and time you left the message in the note space below the task. If you send an e-mail to follow up on an item and are waiting for a reply, make a notation. When you finish a task in its entirety, put the date and time of completion and check it off. If the task becomes unnecessary for any reason, place an "X" over it to indicate it was not completed because of a change in circumstances.

Write on only one side of each sheet of paper in the steno pad. Whenever you have completed all tasks on a page, flip the page up to the cover and rubber band or spring clip it with previously completed pages against the cardboard backing. Only the pages with tasks to be completed are then left free on the pad.

Continue through the pad to the last page, flip the steno pad over, and begin to go back the other way through the pad. Once a pad is entirely completed, label it with the beginning and ending dates on the cover. Rubber band it closed and file it in case you need to verify that a task was completed. Discard the steno pad after an appropriate amount of time has passed without your having to reference it.

TRACKING MISCELLANEOUS TASKS

9/12   Call Karl Fisher about bar luncheon

698-8865

msg 3pm   T/C 4:30pm

___

9/12   Mary needs notes from marketing

committee

___

9/13   Pick up dry cleaning for Andy

___

9/13   Email CLE info to John

___

9/14   Call Joe Mitchell about plane reservation

✳   for Denver

msg 9am   T/C 11am

msg 10:30am

DETERMINING YOUR BEST TIMES FOR MENTAL HEAVY LIFTING

Each lawyer has a personal set of high- and low-energy times for work. Some hours of the day are highly productive with maximum focus. These are the hours when we should do the most difficult and challenging tasks that consume the most energy and require our brains to do heavy lifting. Some hours in the day seem to be plagued by wandering concentration and low energy. These hours should be filled with tasks that are shorter, more routine, and take fewer mental resources. The remaining hours of the workday are somewhere in between these two energy extremes; we can accomplish more than during our low-energy times, but not as much as in our high-energy periods.

If you are not already aware of your energy fluctuations during the day, complete the following exercise. For two weeks, keep track each day of your productivity and energy levels. You can keep track directly on your daily appointment calendar. Place a bracket around or highlight and label the hours each day when you felt most alert and productive. Those time periods are high-energy hours for the day. Next place a bracket around or highlight in a second color and label the hours each day when you felt the least alert and productive. Those time periods are low-energy times. The remaining hours during your workday are your medium-energy hours.

Look for any triggers that caused variations in your energy levels. Did your energy level differ after meetings, after business lunches, or at mid-week? Did your energy level increase or decrease due to a certain administrative task, due to a specific type of drafting project, or when you met with a certain client? Did your energy level vary when you had less sleep or were worried by a family problem?

Look for possible patterns over the two weeks. Were you typically the most productive at the same times of day or on the same days? When were you typically less productive? If you had patterns, plan your work in future weeks with those patterns in mind.

You will want to match the difficulty of your tasks with your energy and productivity levels at different points in the day. Here are some examples of the types of tasks you might consider doing:

- During high-energy periods, tackle writing, researching, or drafting projects. Schedule your meetings on difficult topics and your appointments on challenging cases during these hours. If possible, reserve high-energy hours on your calendar for concentrated work on projects without any interruptions.
- When your energy is at a medium level, review reports, read practice area updates, edit documents, or plan upcoming projects. Meetings or client appointments on more routine matters should occur during these times of day.
- During your low-energy periods, review and respond to routine e-mails, sort through the mail, review and sign letters, or organize materials for a later project. Try to avoid meetings and appointments if possible.

If you are typically in your office throughout the entire workday, you will want to reserve high-energy times for projects as consistently as possible. However, if you are often out of the office for court, depositions, or on-site client visits, you may be able to schedule your high-energy times for projects intentionally only once or twice a week.

KNOW YOUR FIRM'S POLICIES AND YOUR SUPERVISOR'S PREFERENCES

Legal employers vary greatly on their policies about individual work styles. You want to know your law firm's parameters so you do not inadvertently violate some rule during your honest endeavors to work more efficiently and effectively.

Does your firm have any policy regarding open or closed office doors? One firm may require lawyers to meet with clients in conference rooms and have their own office doors open. Another firm may expect office doors to be kept open unless clients are being interviewed in the lawyers' offices. A third firm may encourage lawyers to keep their office doors open as much as possible but realize the need for uninterrupted work time and closed doors.

Firms may have adopted an open-door policy to encourage interaction among all firm members. However, the policy may be abused, as in "you must always be available to me no matter what you are doing." A successful open-door policy should balance interaction with quiet time for concentrated work.

Does your employer have any policy about others fielding your telephone calls or e-mails? Some firms realize that it is more efficient at times for well-trained staff to field lawyers' telephone calls and provide for callbacks unless an important matter arises. Other firms insist on lawyers answering their own telephone calls. The same dichotomy may be true in regard to e-mail messages.

The first type of firm realizes that constant interruptions decrease a lawyer's ability to complete tasks. The second type of firm believes that clients will be impressed if lawyers answer their calls personally. A balance between uninterrupted project time and availability by telephone is probably most realistic for law practices.

Does your firm have any policy about the time span for returning telephone calls or responding to e-mails? Most firms realize that lawyers need some discretion in responding to telephone calls and e-mails. Lawyers need to balance work obligations with the importance of the client matter related to the call or e-mail. By scheduling regular time periods in your day for returning telephone calls and replying to e-mails, you can respond within a reasonable time frame without having constant interruptions.

What are your supervisor's preferences? Once you know your law firm's policies, you also need to know whether your supervisor's preferences are more stringent. Your supervisor may support your time management efforts, even when your strategies differ from the supervisor's own preferred work methods, if you explain how the strategies will make you more productive. You may need to modify some of the suggested strategies in this book to account for your supervisor's style.

AWARENESS OF INTERRUPTIONS TO YOUR WORK

Some of the common interruptions when trying to concentrate on a project are questions from colleagues or staff, drop-in visits by these same people, correspondence needing your signature, telephone calls, e-mails, and text messages. Because daily interruptions become so normal, you may not realize how much time you lose. For each interruption during a project, you must change focus, deal with the interruption, regain your focus (usually by rereading or trying to recapture your thought process prior to the interruption), and then make up for the lost time. The impact is greater than just the interruption time itself because you must also consider the extra time it takes to regain your focus.

If you are not already aware of the common interruptions during your work and the amount of time you lose to them, keep track for one week. Write down the type of interruption, how long the interruption lasted, your work task at the time of the interruption, the impact of the interruption on continuing your task, and the total time lost (interruption plus impact). Finally, note whether the interruption was important, could have waited until later, or was unimportant.

Important interruptions obviously will need to be handled when they occur and are ultimately a good use of your time. However, other interruptions are time deficits that could often be avoided with some foresight. The sample for tracking interruptions included here illustrates how much time can be lost in a day.

PROJECT TIMES AND PROTECTING THOSE TIMES FROM INTERRUPTIONS

Once you have determined your high-energy hours, determine when you can reserve those times on your calendar for projects—the most important items on your daily task list. Choose consistent blocks of high-energy time several times a week (or every day if your job allows it) that will be your uninterrupted time for projects. For those who are controlled by the court docket, it may be easier to reserve time for office projects one day a week when court appearances are less likely.

After determining which of your high-energy time blocks for projects work best within your weekly schedule, explain your new time management strategy to your assigned staff members and any lawyers with whom you work closely. By implementing the same consistent schedule for project time every week, it will be easier for them to anticipate and honor your request for uninterrupted time. If possible within your firm's

● ●

Tracking Interruptions

Date	Type	Time Lost	Task Interrupted	Impact	Total Time Lost	Important?
4/30	Question John	8 minutes	Contract review	15 minutes refocus & rereading	23 minutes	Could wait
	Letters to sign Ronald	2 minutes	Contract review	1 minute refocus	3 minutes	Could wait
	Telephone call librarian	15 minutes	Reading cases for research	Started case over – 20 minutes	35 minutes	Could wait
	Letters to sign Julie	3 minutes	Reading cases for research	5 minutes rereading	8 minutes	Could wait
	Telephone call client	9 minutes	Memo drafting	15 minutes to recapture thoughts	24 minutes	Yes
	Question John	5 minutes	Memo drafting	2 minutes refocus	7 minutes	Could wait
	Question Sharon	4 minutes	Memo drafting	2 minutes refocus	6 minutes	Yes
	Drop-in visit Toby	12 minutes	Contract review	Gave up and went home	12 minutes plus gave up	Totally unimportant – NFL game rehash

During this one day, there were eight interruptions. A total of thirty minutes, which resulted in a good use of time, was given to two important interruptions. A total of seventy-six minutes was lost to five interruptions that could have waited until later. A total of twelve minutes plus giving up and going home resulted from the one nonimportant interruption.

culture, have your staff member field telephone calls and e-mails[6] and keep your door closed during your project time.

---

6. If you do not have a staff member to field your telephone calls during your project time, use voicemail or forward your telephone calls to the receptionist if that is appropriate. If you are a solo practitioner, consider whether an answering service would assist you more than voicemail.

Designate consistent time periods in the morning and afternoon when you will be available to handle routine matters that do not need immediate attention. You can then handle these routine items in a batch rather than intermittently while you are trying to focus your attention on projects. Diplomatically request that your staff and colleagues save routine matters for the designated times. Choose your time periods to handle these routine matters based on the office work flow; match the length and frequency to the needs of your specific practice.

Of course, as mentioned above, some interruptions will be too important to wait. You can give your staff member a list of people who have permission to interrupt you *at any time* (certain clients, your supervisor, opposing counsel on a current case, or others). With scheduled times for your availability for routine matters, staff will be able to take messages from other people, tell them when you will return telephone calls, and suggest that colleagues come back to consult with you at the designated times.

RESERVED TIME WITHIN YOUR WEEKLY SCHEDULE

You will never be able to control everything about your workweek. Therefore, you want to designate at least two blocks of time on your calendar each week as *reserved time* to allow you some maneuverability when it is needed. Reserved time can be used for several types of tasks:

- unexpected projects that land on your desk
- reorganization of your work when an emergency has displaced a scheduled project
- extra time when you have misjudged how long a task will take
- new appointments that need to be scheduled on short notice

If the reserved time is not needed, you simply consult your daily and weekly task lists to see how to use the time constructively. Reserved time can then be used to get ahead on another project, complete reading to update you in your practice area, or finish several administrative tasks.

WHEN CHAOS INTERVENES

Expect days when all your careful planning will be thrown off by a real crisis. Do not react immediately out of a sense of urgency. Take several deep breaths, calmly collect your thoughts, and consider the new development carefully. Determine exactly what it means for your time commitments for the day.

Take a positive attitude toward the development. Tell yourself that you can competently handle the interruption to your plans. Negative emotions will just add to your stress.

Evaluate the magnitude of the crisis. Take a few minutes to find out what you can about the situation before you jump to any conclusions based on the first report. Once you have determined the full nature of the crisis, you can begin to plan your approach.

List on paper the specific tasks that will need to be completed to resolve the new development. For each task, estimate the amount of time required. In addition, list any people who can assist you in completing the tasks.

Now that you have a timeline and task list for handling the crisis, look at your daily task list and appointment calendar. Ask yourself the following questions:

- What items on your daily task list can be moved most easily to later in the day or to another day to make room for the crisis? Consider the task's priority category before you decide whether it can be delayed and for how long.
- What items on your task list could appropriately be assigned to someone else to complete? Consider the other person's familiarity with the matter as well as his or her competency to complete the task.
- Which of your appointments needs to be moved to make room for the crisis? Consider whether someone else could handle the appointment rather than rescheduling it.
- When are blocks of reserved time scheduled on your calendar? Determine whether any tasks or appointments could be moved to those slots and still be completed in a timely fashion.

- Whom do you need to contact in your firm's hierarchy to discuss your decisions about delaying or reassigning tasks, if anyone? Consider whether you have the authority to make these decisions or whether you need to consult with someone more senior.

CAPTURING WINDFALL TIME

During a workday, it is possible to capture time that was originally scheduled but becomes available and can be redistributed for other tasks. A meeting is canceled, which opens up an hour on your calendar. A client decides to come to your office, saving you an hour of travel time. A colleague telephones from the courthouse to say he will be twenty minutes late for your project meeting. Your legal assistant had to take an important telephone call, which gives you ten extra minutes before your scheduled meeting with him.

You may use *windfall time* in several ways. First, you could pick a task from your list that fits the amount of windfall time available and complete that task. Second, you could complete several smaller miscellaneous or administrative tasks (perhaps from your steno-pad task list) that fit into the windfall time. Third, you may be able to move other tasks up or down within your daily schedule to capture the windfall time plus another block of open time together, resulting in a much longer block of task time. Fourth, if you are truly on top of everything, you could take a break and relax!

You will want to consider the types of tasks that might be done in small blocks of windfall time. Here are some examples to consider:

- Use fifteen minutes or less to check your e-mails, straighten up your desk, review and reprioritize your task lists, review and sign routine letters, compose several routine e-mails, or make a short telephone call.
- Use twenty to thirty minutes to review the subsequent history for several cases, check citations in a legal memorandum, compose a short letter to your client, read an article in your reading stack, make a longer telephone call, compose a longer e-mail, visit with a

staff member to review progress on a project, or complete a partial sort of your incoming stack.

- Use forty-five to sixty minutes to prepare for an upcoming meeting, read and brief several judicial opinions for a research project, compose a lengthy client letter, work on an outline for a legal memorandum, edit a document, read multiple articles in your reading stack, or sort your entire incoming stack.

Windfall time can get frittered away if you do not have a stock of tasks that you know will fit time blocks of an hour or less. If you capture just thirty minutes of windfall time each day for five workdays, you have found two and a half extra hours to complete tasks.

THE BILLING CONNECTION TO TIME MANAGEMENT

If your work will be billed to a client on an hourly-fee basis, you want to be conscientious in capturing your billing units. You want the bill to be accurate and not overlook units that you need for your billing target. Record billing units at the time you complete the task whenever possible. Reconstructing your tasks and time after the fact is much harder and often means lost billing units.

Recording your billing units at the time of the work also allows you to incorporate sufficient details while the tasks are still fresh in your mind. You want to produce an informative invoice. "Telephone call with client summarizing research about water rights for the Henderson property" is more desirable than "telephone call with client." Your supervisor also needs sufficient information when finalizing the client's invoice as to the specific work completed and whether any time should be discounted. Clients are less likely to dispute charges accompanied by detailed explanations for the completed work.

Enter all your time spent on a task rather than determining yourself whether it will ultimately be billed to the client. Your supervisor will review the client invoice and discount time where necessary. If you have undertaken work that should have been completed by a lower-fee staff member, you need to delegate those tasks in the future. If you have consistently overworked on tasks, you need to evaluate your time and work management strategies.

Alternative fee arrangements have become more prevalent. Clients gain greater certainty regarding legal costs, and firms gain flexibility in assigning work if they are adept at setting fees. Firms need experience to set alternative fees at profitable levels. Consequently, these firms may still require lawyers to capture time so they have accurate data for adjusting future fee arrangements.

Lawyers who work for legal employers who do not bill clients are freed from billing targets and the drudgery of timekeeping. However, their employers may substitute other measures, such as the number of matters completed or timeliness of completion. As a result, skills at time and work management will still be important.

Whatever your legal position, you will be of greater value to your employer if you turn out work in an efficient and effective manner. No employer will be satisfied with a lawyer who takes too long to complete every project or who is unable to prioritize projects correctly. Wise management of your time and work can protect your continued employment.

Reflection and Strategies

1. If you formulated professional goals for the year during your firm's performance review process, are you satisfied with your progress toward those goals? If not, what are the obstacles to meeting those goals? How can you lessen the impact of those obstacles or remove them entirely?

2. Schedule time on your calendar to review any predetermined goals and to set any additional professional goals. For each goal, write down the strategies and tasks for implementing the goal.

3. What goals would make you more valuable to your employer?
4. What goals would make you more efficient in your work?
5. What goals would make your more effective in your work?
6. Which strategies could you implement to streamline handling your mail and other incoming/outgoing items?
7. Evaluate the high-, medium-, and low-energy times during your workday and week. Determine which job tasks are most appropriate to complete during each of those times.
8. How well do you currently prioritize your projects and tasks? What methods could you adopt to improve in this area?
9. What are the most common interruptions in your workday, and how do you currently deal with them? Consider strategies to minimize those interruptions and increase your productivity while still being responsive to staff members and clients.
10. How well do you handle crises during your workday? What strategies can you implement to manage crises effectively while minimizing the disruption to your day?

How to Deal with Competing Demands on Your Time

Control over your day will depend on your type of legal work, your legal employer, and the work distribution system at your firm. Whatever your environment, however, you will be confronted with competing demands from partners, other lawyers, clients, and project deadlines. In order to flourish rather than just survive, you must prioritize and organize projects for timely completion.

Confirm who has the ultimate decision-making power over your work. The ideal situation is having just one supervisor to please. This supervisor determines your workload, any deadlines, work formats, and expectations. When you are asked to take on projects for other lawyers, your supervisor can resolve any conflicts in priorities and deadlines.

If you report to several supervisors, it is inevitable that you will have work with conflicting deadlines. In those situations, ask your supervisors to resolve any conflicts and direct you as to the new priorities. Do not make the mistake of trying to determine yourself which project comes first—you will risk pleasing one person and irritating another.

Realize that there may be office politics that you do not know about. There are often personality conflicts, power struggles, and pecking orders within a legal office, and such issues may be unknown to a lawyer who was hired after those dynamics developed. Others may know the subtext, while you will take instructions at face value and be unable to read between the lines.

If you are caught in the middle of office politics, realize that the matter is all about the individuals at odds and not about you personally. Remain neutral, stay diplomatic, and avoid causing offense. If your supervisor is not involved in the conflict, explain the problem and ask the supervisor for advice. Leave the matter with the supervisor to resolve and get back to you with a decision.

Create a project list to track all assignments. You always need to stay very aware of your work flow for multiple assignments. You do not want to become immersed in one project and consequently mismanage your time for another one.

In addition to the monthly, weekly, and daily task lists that you create,[1] you will need a project list to see the overview of the multiple projects you are juggling. By glancing at your project list, you can quickly monitor your progress on multiple deadlines.[2]

The following items should be included on your overview project list:

- date the assignment was made
- person for whom the assignment is being done
- type/format of assignment (memorandum, brief, interrogatory, contract)
- client reference (name and client file number)
- deadline (or multiple deadlines for stages within the project and what is due on each date)
- comments on the assignment (estimated time to be spent, billable status, permission for electronic research, sources recommended, notes from conference)
- assigning lawyer's preferred method of contact for later questions or updates (e-mail, voicemail, appointment, memo)
- additional instructions for the project
- completion date (or multiple completion dates for stages within the project)

As soon as you know there is a conflict in deadlines for a new assignment, make it known to the assigning lawyer. Your overview project list may alert you to the conflict at the time you are in the initial discussion about the project. In that case, alert the assigning lawyer to your inability to meet the proposed deadline—or even that you are unable to take on the project within your current workload. Should the assignment come to you without a chance for discussion, or you

---

1. Chapter 4 discussed monthly, weekly, and daily task lists; refer to that chapter if you need more information.
2. Depending on your circumstances, you can use a database, spreadsheet, Word table, or preprinted forms for your overview project list.

Project List

Date Assigned	Assigned By	Type of Assignment	Client Ref.	Deadline	Comments	Contact	Additional	Date Done
2/1	John Smithson	Research	Ravi file 2012-886-1	2/7	Talk with John about findings	Make 2/8 appt. with John		2/5
2/8	Mac Johnson	Memo	Jones file 2012-458-5	2/18 First Issue 2/24 Second Issue	No $ for electronic research	Make appt. if Qs	Tim Collins has pre-2009 experience on Issue 2	
2/9	Sarah Maxwell	Affidavit	Sanchez file 2012-967-1	2/16		E-mail her		2/14
2/14	John Smithson	Client letter re: research findings	Ravi file 2012-886-1	2/22	Show John before meeting	Leave message w/Gail re: review	Arrange meeting w/ client & Smithson	

discover after the fact that you have a conflict, again alert the assigning lawyer immediately. When there is early notice, an assigning lawyer can more easily rethink a deadline or find someone else to do the work.

Confirm deadlines for any assignment in writing whenever possible. Follow up any lengthy discussion about a newly assigned project with an e-mail confirming your understanding of the assignment and the deadline. If your assignment was given to you by memorandum or e-mail rather than in person, reply that you will undertake the assignment (assuming you can do so with your other projects) and confirm the deadline. If you have additional questions about the assignment to include in the same confirmation e-mail, change the original subject heading to alert the reader that you are asking for additional information. If you have to decline the assignment, it is preferable to do so in a face-to-face meeting and explain your reasons.

Set an artificial deadline for a project at least two days prior to the actual deadline. By working toward the earlier deadline, you will have extra time for a final edit, correction of citation errors, or format changes. In addition, you will not be as stressed if there are unforeseen problems near the deadline: you get ill, your legal assistant resigns, or the computer system crashes. If you have several projects due on the same day, stagger your artificial deadlines to allow more time: one project two days earlier, one project four days earlier, and so forth. Use a monthly calendar to map out deadlines, artificial deadlines, and meetings related to your assignments.

Estimate the time needed on each project. Consider the tasks that will have to be completed within the project. Estimate how long you will need for each task. If you are unsure, estimate a range. Take the higher number within that range and add 20 percent to get your estimated total time for the task. Then add all task estimates to have your estimated time for the entire project.

Consider the following items as you estimate your time for a project:

- your background and expertise in the legal practice area
- difficulty of the actual assignment for you
- complexity of the project
- other people with whom you will have to confer in order to complete the project (and possible delays on their part because of conflicting priorities)
- any missing information needed before you can begin the project
- any unique aspects about the project

It is better to estimate too much time than to underestimate and run out of time. If you finish ahead of your estimate, you can just move on to the next task or project. See the sample project estimate sheet provided.

Use the estimates for tasks to schedule the entire project on a calendar.[3] This distribution of tasks visually confirms whether you can actually complete the project to meet your deadline as you planned. By adding the tasks for multiple projects to the same calendar, you can see clearly whether there are any bottlenecks that you were previously unaware of in your planning. For example, you may discover that two

---

3. You could also use project management software to accomplish this step for each project and then view multiple projects together. The software will likely include the capability to use color-coded Gantt charts in order to visualize the projects.

Estimate Jones File

ISSUE 1:

Background research: 4 hours

Billable research for Issue 1: 2 days

Draft memo for Issue 1: 2 days

Edits: 4 hours

Total Estimate Issue 1: 5 days

ISSUE 2:

Read memo by Tim Collins: 2 hours

Meeting w/Tim Collins: ½ hour

Update 2009 research: 5½ hours

Draft memo for Issue 2: 1½ days

Edits: 3½ hours

Total Estimate Issue 2: 3 days

Total Project Estimate: 8 days

projects with different deadlines are in fact problematic because the workload required at several stages within each separate project cannot be accomplished simultaneously.

If you discover problems that cannot be resolved by rescheduling individual tasks, you need to talk with the assigning lawyers or your supervisor as soon as possible. By alerting everyone to the problems quickly, new deadlines can be determined or the work reassigned with the least disruption. A sample monthly calendar with assignments is provided.

Deal proactively with projects without specific deadlines. At times you may receive projects without hard and fast deadlines. These projects come in two main types. First, a project may be more hypothetical in nature. These assignments are basically the "it's just a matter

• •

Monthly Calendar with Assignments

("AD" indicates an artificial deadline)

FEBRUARY						
Monday	Tuesday	Wednesday	Thursday	Friday	Saturday	Sunday
	1 AD: Final edit Lowe memo	**2** Research Ravi	**3** DEADLINE LOWE Research Ravi	**4** Finalize Ravi findings	**5** AD: Complete Ravi	**6**
7 DEADLINE RAVI 5 pm	**8** 9:00 Lowe Meeting 3:00 Meeting Smithson	**9** Review Sanchez file Research Jones 1	**10** Draft Sanchez Research Jones 1	**11** Draft Sanchez Research Jones 1	**12** Draft Jones 1	**13**
14 Draft Jones 1 Edit Sanchez AD: Finish Sanchez	**15** Read Collins 2009 memo 11:00 Tim Collins Edit Jones 1	**16** DEADLINE SANCHEZ AD: Finish Jones 1 Final edit Jones 1	**17** Draft Ravi letter Research Jones 2	**18** DEADLINE JONES 1 Draft Ravi Research & start draft Jones 2	**19** AD: Finish Ravi letter Edit Ravi Draft Jones 2	**20**
21 Draft Jones 2 Final edit Ravi if needed	**22** DEADLINE Ravi AD: Jones 2 Edit Jones 2	**23** Final edit Jones 2 if needed	**24** DEADLINE Jones 2 3:00 Ravi meeting	**25**	**26**	**27**
28						

of time" questions that one knows will need to be answered but does not know when. For example, a lawyer may want to know what the law would be if his client decides to implement a particular company policy later in the year.

Second, an assigning lawyer may have an unspoken deadline in mind but not mention it because the client is not demanding immediate attention. The lawyer may tell you to complete the assignment "when you get to it" but really mean "by the end of next week," because in his mind that is more than enough time for you to complete the work and for him to respond to the client.

The tendency is to leave assignments without specific deadlines on the back burner and focus only on the tasks with definite deadlines. However, it is always wiser to suggest a deadline and confirm if that deadline will work for the assigning lawyer. If the assigning lawyer disagrees with your suggested timeline, you will gain clarification up front and not be ambushed by an unexpected deadline later.

When suggesting a deadline, consider the following matters to fit these assignments in with your definite-deadline projects:

- Consider the difficulty and complexity of the project. If the project is difficult or extensive, completing it in small stages throughout work on other projects may be wise. If it can be completed fairly quickly, you may want to slip it in after the completion of one project deadline and before the next project begins—especially if the two-days-before artificial deadline has given you a breather between two projects.
- Consider any missing information on the project. If you will need time to gather information before undertaking the project, you may wish to begin doing so early in preparation for the main work to be completed.

Know when you can simultaneously work on several projects and when you cannot. Do not treat all projects equally. Know when you need to focus solely on one project until it is completed and when you will be able to work on several deadlines at once.

Sometimes it is easy to switch between different projects because each task is discreet and uncomplicated. You quickly recover your train of thought, keep facts and details straight, and effectively manage both projects. Other projects are so complex that you will waste huge amounts of time getting your focus back if you jump between them.

Competing demands are a fact of life in the practice of law. You will work for a variety of assigning lawyers with different expectations and styles. You will need to adapt and learn the most efficient and effective ways to complete your projects for each person. Your success will depend on how you organize your multiple projects and manage your time to meet deadlines.

Reflection and Strategies

1. How common is it for you to end up with competing demands on your time? How do you currently handle those conflicts?
2. What different strategies could you implement to manage your projects and assignments better than you are currently doing?
3. Do you procrastinate on projects because you think you work better under pressure or because you do not have a definite deadline to meet? If so, how might you handle projects more effectively to avoid procrastination?

How to Manage Staff Effectively, Ask for Assistance, and Delegate

Whether you have internal or external support staff working with you, you need to manage them efficiently and effectively. Internal staff may include secretaries, paralegals, legal assistants, librarians, document assembly technicians, or others. External staff may include contract lawyers, a transcription service, or couriers. Your interaction with staff can streamline your job or create obstacles.

GENERAL POINTS ABOUT WORKING WITH STAFF

Treat all support staff with respect and collegiality. Support staff members are the backbone of any legal employer. They impact the speed, accuracy, and quality with which tasks are completed. They often choose which tasks get completed first when there are no deadlines to determine the order. Because their work is critical to your tasks, you need to treat staff as team members rather than as mere subordinates.

Some lawyers become impressed with their own positions and importance. If you are one of them, you need an attitude adjustment. As a new lawyer, you may have an outstanding law school résumé; however, you are just another lawyer until you prove yourself. Even after you become a senior associate or partner, you will have even greater future success if you remember that others helped you attain and maintain your success.

Here are some tips for forming a positive relationship with staff members:

- Take the time to learn staff names and how to pronounce them correctly.
- If you work regularly with a staff member, learn about his or her family members and ask after them when appropriate. Long discussions are not necessary. Good manners, however, indicate that you consider the staff member as a person rather than merely a position.

- Remain professional at all times when dealing with staff members. Do not participate in office gossip by initiating it or listening to it.
- Answer any follow-up queries from staff promptly so they are not stalled on your project because they need additional information. If you are going to be out of the office while they complete a project, provide staff with contact information.
- Say "please" and "thank you" as appropriate when staff members assist you. If you are asking a staff person to go above and beyond the job description, acknowledge that you are doing so.
- If a mistake is made, calmly explain the error and ask that the task be redone. Control your temper; shouting will not win you points with that staff member for the next time you need assistance.
- Realize the power of the office grapevine. Every other staff member for your employer will hear about your good or bad behavior as a supervisor. Depending on your reputation, staff will or will not be eager to help you with projects.

Recognize your own strengths. Each of us has certain talents, skills, and abilities. Consider the tasks that most frequently appear in the most important category on your weekly and daily task lists.[1] As much as possible, increase the time you spend on your most important tasks that showcase your strengths and provide you with positive feedback. Then consider the tasks that most frequently appear in the important category on your task lists. Showcase your strengths whenever possible with these tasks as well. If you have strengths that are currently not used in your position, seek opportunities to use those strengths within the firm when appropriate. For example, volunteer for a project or committee that would benefit from your expertise.

Recognize your own weaknesses. Each of us also has areas that are not our strong points. A task may require a set of skills you do not possess. Or a task may just be new to you, and you need some guidance

---

1. See Chapter 4 at pages 30–32 for a discussion of most important, important, and least important task categories.

the first time. Whatever the reason for a weakness, own up to it and get assistance. Do not try to bluff your colleagues into thinking that you can do something well that you cannot do. Do not let pride prevent you from asking someone else to work with you on a task. Be open to learning from others and expanding your skills.

Realize that a staff member may know more than you do about certain tasks. Do not underestimate staff expertise. If you are a new lawyer, new to your firm, or a first-time supervisor, be prepared to learn from staff members who have competently handled tasks for many years. An experienced paralegal, legal assistant, or law librarian will have a wealth of information to benefit you. Other long-term staff members, whether file clerks, document assembly technicians, or supply clerks, can recommend the most effective and efficient ways to complete their aspects of your work. Respect staff members' experience while still maintaining your ultimate responsibility as a supervisor.

Know the strengths and weaknesses of staff members. To get maximum results from staff members, initially assume that they genuinely want to help you and are competent to do so. As you get to know each staff member, use their strengths to advantage, remember their weaknesses, and rely on those who are willing and able to help you succeed.

Make your expectations clear from the beginning. Staff members cannot read your mind. Tell them what you consider important about your workday and work products. Whether it is the font you prefer used in drafts, the information you want in your telephone messages, or the organization of your client files, *you* need to delineate your preferences. Every supervisor is different, so do not assume that staff will realize your idiosyncrasies and pet peeves.

Ask for suggestions on how you can be more effective and efficient in your own work. Once you have built a rapport with staff members, ask for honest feedback on your own work style. Be open to suggestions on how to streamline tasks, coordinate your work with the staff member, or have the staff member assist you in new ways.

Also ask for feedback on things that you do unintentionally that make the staff member's job more difficult. We all have quirks and inefficiencies that we are unaware of; however, they are often obvious to another person. It takes a mature person to listen to constructive comments and make adjustments. Your staff member can become an indispensable ally and colleague if you allow that type of professional relationship to develop.

Remember where the buck stops. Whenever you are the supervising lawyer for a task or project, you are ultimately responsible for the quality and timeliness of the work product. You need to calendar dates when delegated staff tasks are due back to you. You need to review all project tasks carefully for accuracy and completeness.

Do not be tempted to place the blame for failure elsewhere. "I was given the project late" or "Joe didn't give me enough information" are ultimately excuses for *your* decisions regarding your work. You could have asked for extra clerical assistance if the upcoming deadline required it. You could have followed up with Joe for more information. Instead of blaming others, recognize your own weaknesses in managing a project and determine how you will manage future projects differently to avoid repeating your mistakes.

Reward your staff members for quality work. Make sure that you say "thank you" often and share the glory for successful completion of tasks. Always give credit where it is due. If staff members have added to the success of a major project, thank them personally and, if possible, publicly. If staff members know they are appreciated and part of a team, they will be more amenable to working with you on future projects.

Discuss privately with staff members any problem areas in their work. When a staff member is underperforming, discuss the problem at an appropriate time. Choose a time when (1) you can remain calm during the discussion, (2) the discussion can take place away from others, and (3) you will have sufficient time for a thorough discussion without interruptions. Prior to the discussion, be honest as to any part you have played in creating a bad situation rather than assuming that only the staff member is to blame. Explain the problem as you see it and your expectations. Listen to the staff member's observations and allow time for questions.

Work constructively with the staff member to seek a mutual solution whenever possible. Give the staff member a chance to fix the deficiencies if the person is willing and capable of doing so.

Document the discussion for your own files (date, main points, and agreed-on performance changes). Depending on the seriousness of the problem, you may need to confer with your human resources staff before and after the discussion. You will want to know your employer's policies and procedures for supervisors.

GENERAL POINTS ABOUT ASKING FOR ASSISTANCE

Everyone needs help at times. Unfortunately, some lawyers find it very hard to ask for assistance. They view the lawyer's role as always having the right answer, being the ultimate authority, and impressing others with brilliance.

You will need to ask for help. And you will need to be smart enough to ask for help *before* you are in major trouble on a project and to ask for assistance from the people best situated to provide it.

Remember your obligations to the firm and your client. If you get a case or project that is out of your comfort zone or you are struggling to finish on time, you owe it professionally to your employer and client to ask for assistance. Swallow your pride and ask for whatever help is needed.

Determine your employer's available means of assistance. What lines of communication exist in your practice area and elsewhere in the firm when you have a procedural question, a drafting difficulty, or an administrative problem? Know both the official sources of assistance as well as the go-to people at your firm. In a large firm, you will have more options: practice manager, administrative staff, law librarians, secretaries, paralegals, legal assistants, and other lawyers. In smaller legal environments, you will quickly recognize the people to whom everyone turns for help on different matters.

Become familiar with the lawyers in your firm. Learn about their specialty areas and other expertise. These are the folks that you are most likely to interact with on a regular basis. Make a mental note of which lawyers you think would be good resources for you. If possible, find at least one mentor among the more experienced lawyers.

Introduce yourself to all the nonlawyers at your firm. Get to know the law librarians, secretaries, paralegals, legal assistants, receptionists, document assembly staff, mailroom staff, janitorial staff, and security guards. These folks have a wealth of practical expertise and firm knowledge that can make your existence easier.

Be astute as to who are the sincere helpers. It is natural for people to say, "Let me know if I can do anything for you." Most people sincerely mean it. Some do not. It is your job to determine which ones do mean it.

Make a mental note when someone says that they are willing to help. Then watch how they interact with the people who work for and with them. Are they approachable? Are they helpful? Do they treat staff and lawyers equally well? Do you overhear complaints about them or praise? Your observations will help you decide whether that person is someone you want to approach when *you* need assistance.

Try the person out on something small when it seems appropriate. Did the person seem happy to assist? Did the person seem too harried to have the time to help? Did the person actually tell you the correct information or procedure?

Carefully evaluate what type of help you need. When you can express your specific need succinctly, it will be easier for someone to assist you. Do you need specific information to finish a task? Do you need someone's expertise on just one procedural aspect of a project? Do you need insight into a client's business? Do you need advice on an ethical issue? Do you need administrative or clerical assistance?

Consider your own willingness to delegate and your experience with delegation. Lawyers who as law students studied alone and depended on themselves to learn everything may be leery of delegating work. They may have had unsatisfactory experiences with small group assignments or study groups that added to their tendency to do everything without assistance. Any lawyer who prefers to be in total control or is a perfectionist may also be hesitant to delegate to others.

If you resist delegation for these or other reasons, you must be honest with yourself about when you truly do not need any help and when you are merely refusing to request the help you need. If you work excessive overtime to meet deadlines or have to ask for time extensions on a regular basis to finish your work, you likely need to delegate some tasks to others so that you can concentrate on the most important tasks on your desk.

Some newer lawyers have no prior experience delegating tasks and monitoring their delegation for successful results because they were never in prior employment situations where they supervised others. Instead they were completing work delegated to them by everyone else. These lawyers will have legitimate questions about how they should delegate work for the best results.

STEPS FOR EFFECTIVE DELEGATION

In learning to delegate, begin slowly. Choose moderately small tasks, choose staff members whom you trust, and allow plenty of time for their completion of the tasks. Here are the steps that are pertinent to delegation:

- Determine whether a task is appropriate for delegation.
- Choose the best person to complete the task.
- Consider the proper timing for the delegation.
- Provide for any necessary discussion regarding the delegation.
- Communicate clearly about the assignment's details.
- Follow up on the delegated tasks.
- Evaluate the completed work product from the delegation.

Determine whether a task is appropriate for delegation. There are potentially three types of tasks that you might delegate: tasks you do not like doing, tasks you know someone else is better at doing than you are, and specific tasks within a larger project on which you are working. The first two types of delegation tend to be permanent. The third type of delegation tends to be temporary in nature.

When considering delegating tasks that you do not like doing, think through the following points before making the delegation. The decision may be more difficult than you think it is.

- Ask yourself whether the tasks you plan to delegate are an integral part of your job description and duties. If so, you may be giving away tasks that are the reason your employer hired you and pays your salary.
- Ask yourself whether the tasks you plan to delegate are appropriate for someone else to be doing. As your client load increases, it is natural to want to delegate certain tasks to paralegals or law clerks. However, keep in mind the complexity of the tasks, the ability levels of those staff members, and your supervisory responsibilities if you delegate.
- Realize that clients will not always be pleased to find that you are no longer handling all tasks personally. Discussion beforehand with clients about your continued supervision of the case, the cost savings of tasks being delegated to lower-hourly-rate fee earners, and your trust in the people who are assigned work will likely resolve any client concerns.
- Ask yourself whether the tasks you plan to delegate are ones that you have authority to delegate. Just because you do not like certain tasks does not mean you can unilaterally decide to delegate them. There may be administrative or policy reasons why the tasks have not been previously assigned to other people.
- If you need to get permission to delegate tasks, plan how you will present your case to the decision maker. How does the delegation allow you to focus on more important tasks, save time, cut costs, or improve the work product?

If you consider delegating tasks that someone else is better at doing than you are, consider several things in addition to those mentioned already:

- If the tasks are not stand alone, ask yourself how the tasks you are delegating fit with the tasks you are retaining. For the delegation to be successful, you will need to coordinate tasks carefully. For example, if your paralegal is excellent at editing for grammar and punctuation, you will have to coordinate your writing tasks with those editing tasks to allow sufficient time for both of you to complete your own work.

- Ask yourself whether the improvement in the final work product warrants the delegation. If the difference in quality or timeliness is negligible, the delegation may not be worthwhile, especially if coordination will be difficult between the delegated and retained tasks.
- Acknowledge when you delegate the task that you consider the other person to be superior at it. The accolade will provide more willingness to accept the new task and the incentive to do a good job.
- Consider whether the other person's workload allows time to take on the additional tasks. Overloading another person is not a beneficial outcome and merely reallocates a problem rather than solving it.

If you are delegating specific tasks that you do not have time to do because of the complexity or short timeline of an overall project, then think through the following aspects:

- Consider which tasks can be delegated without negatively impacting the project's overall quality. Delegate tasks that either allow you more time to work on the most important aspects of the project or distribute the work in a way that will ensure timeliness and quality control.
- Calculate very good time estimates for all the tasks in the project. Determine which important tasks you can realistically complete yourself and which tasks will require delegation.
- Delegate tasks as soon as possible to allow others plenty of time to complete their work.
- Anticipate any coordination problems that might occur. Allow time to update all team members on the project timeline and their duties. Determine how to fit your tasks smoothly with their tasks.

Choose the best person to complete the task. Carefully choose the people to whom you delegate tasks. Consider the following before you select the person who will handle a task:

- Determine the skills, talents, and abilities needed for the task you want to delegate, and match the person to those criteria. Ask the staff whiz at numbers to double-check the computations in a report. Ask the staff expert on researching corporate intelligence data to research a defendant corporation.
- Consider the standard you are expecting for the result and determine which individuals have the experience, knowledge, and professional maturity to complete the task to that level.
- List the characteristics that a person needs to complete the task the way you want it done. If the task requires attention to minute details, do not choose a big-picture person. If you need a fast turnaround time, do not choose a staff member who is late on every assignment.
- Decide the amount of time the staff member needs for the delegated task. If the project needs only six hours this week, choose someone who has that amount of time currently available. If you are delegating a task permanently, choose a staff member who has the requisite amount of time available over the long term.

Consider the proper timing for the delegation. Whenever possible, give staff notice when you know there will be an upcoming project on which you expect to need assistance. In addition, estimate the time frame for when you will need help, so staff can then plan their own work more effectively and be available to work on your task.

Plan out each project so that you can clearly foresee whose assistance will be needed for completion, which steps of the project you will retain, and which steps you will delegate.

- A delay in the delegation may be needed to allow time for the staff member to complete other projects. Or the task may need to be delegated in stages instead of all at one time.

- Finish your own work on the project with enough lead time so that you can give the next task to staff early rather than as a rush job.

- Alternatively, if a delegated task is not dependent on first completing another step in the process, delegate it at the very beginning of the project. If the staff member finishes early, you will be that much ahead on your planned timeline.

- Set a deadline for staff tasks at least two days before you actually need the completed tasks from them. This lead time is especially important if you are working with a staff member for the first time or on a complicated project that needs coordination of multiple tasks with multiple people. By allowing extra time in the process, you will be able to integrate all project tasks, handle unexpected problems, complete any remaining tasks of your own, and make necessary adjustments to the final work product without deadline pressure.

Provide for any necessary discussion regarding the delegation. The amount of discussion needed before delegation will vary with the circumstances. Are you delegating a task permanently or temporarily? Is the task already within a person's job description or an additional task? How complex is the delegated task? In several of these scenarios, you would likely get a more positive response if you discussed the assignment with the staff member rather than merely ordering its completion. Consider the following points:

- Minor or routine tasks can typically be delegated by an e-mail or voicemail message. However, requests for rushed service, special favors, or complex tasks are better made in person.

- If you need someone else's authority to delegate the task, plan that discussion. Explain how the delegation will benefit the firm by allowing you to focus on more important tasks, save time, cut costs, or improve the work product.

- Include the person to whom you wish to delegate a new job duty or permanent task in your decision making whenever possible.

- Do not just assume the person will happily accept the additional task. The person may not wish to take on the task for very legitimate reasons of which you are unaware.
- If a staff member's concerns cannot be resolved and the delegation still occurs, there will be fewer hard feelings if you have listened and acknowledged the concerns.

Communicate clearly about the assignment's details. Essential time is wasted when you assign tasks without proper instructions, deadlines, or the necessary materials for completion. You know the what, when, and how of the project; however, your staff member will not know unless you provide the details. Carefully think through the steps that you want staff to complete so you can anticipate the information they will need. Some pointers for good communication include the following:

- Give clear, detailed, and accurate instructions for any complicated task so staff can understand your request completely.
- Many people have trouble with oral instructions, even when they take notes. They are simultaneously trying to listen, write notes, understand the project, and formulate questions. If you hurry through the explanation, something will inevitably be missed, either by you or the staff member.
- You are more likely to mention all steps and important details if you write out the instructions for complicated projects. Your staff member will be better able to complete all steps accurately with the aid of written instructions for reference.
- For written instructions, you will want to use a project delegation form like the sample form included below. The amount of detail in the instructions will depend on the complexity of the project and the staff person's experience level.
- Summarize orally what the instructions say, give the person time to look through the accompanying materials, and then provide time to answer any questions. If the task is very complicated, sug-

gest that you return later to discuss the project after the staff member has had time to review all the information.

- If you need to leave a complex task for someone and cannot meet face-to-face, be sure that your written instructions are adequate. If the person has not done a similar project for you previously, you will need to give more detailed instructions.

• •

Project Delegation Form

Date assigned _____

Deadline date _____

Project description _____

_____

_____

Client file name _____

Client file number _____

_____ Billable   _____ Not billable

Specific instructions:

Follow up on the delegated tasks. This step assumes that the delegated task is either part of a larger project for which you are responsible or you are responsible for supervision of a permanently delegated task. Here are some thoughts on follow-up:

- For a really large or important project, follow up twenty-four to forty-eight hours after leaving the project with the staff member. Simply ask if there are any new questions you need to answer.

- Do not become a control freak or micromanager and constantly ask about the status of the project. If you monitor every detail and constantly interrupt the staff member's work, you ultimately would have been better off doing the task yourself. Also, by asking staff members if they have remembered to do things they obviously have the experience and competence to accomplish, you will signal that you do not trust their intelligence and professionalism.
- Use a project delegation chart like the sample below to track your delegated tasks. The chart should include:
  - the project name
  - the assignment date
  - the people assigned to work on the project
  - the tasks assigned to each person
  - work products required at each deadline
  - deadlines for each work product
  - any other comments needed
- Include all follow-up deadlines on your calendar to make sure that the work products are completed on time.
- Depending on the task delegated and the experience of the staff member, you may want to send reminders regarding the deadlines involved.

Project Delegation Chart

Project	Delegated to and Date Delegated	Tasks Delegated	Work Product Required	Deadlines	Comments
Macmillan File	2/22 Joe Blair	Issue 1 Research	Meeting to discuss project Memo re: Research	3/1 3/8	Told to talk with Glenda about case file
Macmillan File	2/24 Charlotte Collins	Issue 2 Research	Meeting to discuss project Memo re: Research	3/3 3/10	Gave citation to Fallon case and told about Tarleton treatise

- Review the work product immediately after the completion date so that any problem areas can be resolved quickly. Your prompt review is especially important if another task within the project will be impacted.
- Provide feedback to the staff member after the project is completed. Begin with the good points. Make constructive suggestions for improvement if appropriate. Be sure to thank the person for the assistance.

Evaluate the completed work product from the delegation. If you are thoughtful about which tasks to delegate, choose the right people, give accurate instructions, allow sufficient time, and ask for periodic updates, you should rarely need to worry about the work product that is returned to you by a staff member. Consider the following should serious problems with the quality of the work product occur:

- Assuming that you gave a staff member an artificial deadline two days earlier than you really needed the task completed, you may still have sufficient time to correct any errors and rectify the situation.
- Determine whether you need other people on staff to help you fix the work product and avert a missed deadline. If so, quickly request their help in resolving the problems.
- If necessary, get advice from someone senior to you on how to avoid a possible failure on the project. It is better to admit that there is a problem and seek help than to stay silent and let disaster strike.
- If there are repercussions, be professional in your manner. Make it clear that you have learned from your mistake in delegation/supervision and that it will not happen again.

If you are in serious doubt about whether a task should be delegated, then do not delegate. If you are concerned whether a person is up to the task, then consider delegating a different, less important task as a trial run before you go for a high-stakes delegation. You will become a better delegator as you gain experience in your supervisory skills.

....

Reflection and Strategies

1. What are your strengths and weaknesses when you consider each of your assigned job duties?
2. Consider the skills, talents, abilities, strengths, and weaknesses for each of the staff members working with you on a regular basis. Do you need to reevaluate the assigned tasks, the level of responsibility given, or your level of supervision for anyone in light of those aspects?
3. What characteristics would you look for in hiring a new staff member if your goal was to hire someone who complements, rather than duplicates, your own strengths and weaknesses?
4. If you avoid asking for assistance even when you know you should do so, what are the reasons for that avoidance?
5. Consider the seven steps for effective delegation, determine your strengths and weaknesses for each, and implement strategies to improve your delegation skills:
    a. Choosing tasks appropriate for delegation
    b. Choosing the best person to complete the delegated task
    c. Determining the proper timing for delegation
    d. Providing necessary discussion regarding the delegation
    e. Communicating clearly about the assignment
    f. Following up with the staff member about the delegated tasks
    g. Evaluating the completed work product and handling any problems
6. If you were to overhear staff members' comments about you as a supervisor, what would they be saying and would you be pleased or embarrassed?

....

Basic Parameters for Research and Writing Projects

Lawyers spend a large portion of their professional lives researching and writing. For newer lawyers, much of that work may be assigned to them by others. But whether the project is for one's own client matters or those assigned, it is important to organize the work carefully and manage one's time well.

GENERAL POINTERS

Always be prepared to receive an assignment. A pen and pad should be standard items you take to meetings. Take careful notes; do not depend on your memory alone. You want to impress the assigning lawyer with your organization and preparedness. Know the relevant, information-gathering questions to ask for the typical projects you handle. You can minimize follow-up questions if you are well prepared initially.

Communicate as appropriate with the assigning lawyer during your project. Find out whether the lawyer requires updates on your progress. One lawyer will want updating e-mails at periodic intervals. Another lawyer will not expect anything from you until the project deadline.

Also learn the lawyer's preferred method for follow-up if you need further instructions while you work on the project. Lawyers vary on whether they desire e-mails, voicemails, or actual appointments.

Confirm through your calendar and project list that you can complete the assignment as scheduled. If you use the project list and task scheduling techniques described in Chapter 5, you can easily determine problems because of conflicting deadlines. If a conflict is discovered at the time the assignment is made, let the assigning lawyer know immediately so a new deadline can be arranged or the work can be reassigned. A lawyer would rather know at the start that you are unable to accept an assignment than have deadline problems surface later. Also, if an unexpected delay arises during a project, consult your assigning lawyer immediately.

ORGANIZING YOUR RESEARCH

The following questions will assist you in gathering information for typical research projects when the assigning lawyer does not automatically provide everything. As you become more experienced in your practice area and with your firm's procedures, you will no longer need to ask some of these questions because you will be certain about the answers. Questions to consider include the following:

- What work product does the assigning lawyer expect to receive: a written memorandum, an oral report, a client letter, or another format?
- What interim deadlines and final deadline are required for the project?
- What is an overview of the client matter (to provide you with context for your specific research within the case)?
- What are the specific issues that the lawyer wants you to research?
- If you are already aware of potential side issues related to those specific issues, does the lawyer want you to research those side issues as well?
- Are there any additional instructions: the amount of time to be spent on a project, particular sources to be reviewed, or other directions?
- If the firm does not have a standard policy on electronic research (or a flat-fee database contract), what dollar/time/database parameters should you observe for subscription databases?
- If the matter is billable in whole or in part, what are the correct client billing details?

Do not make assumptions based on prior experiences. If you are new to a firm, determine the procedures, policies, resources, and formats for research and writing assignments. Legal employers vary greatly on their parameters. Even within the same firm, assigning lawyers may have different preferences. Determine the following list of specifics for your research project unless you know what your supervisors and firm expect:

- standard format used for office memoranda of law or other work products
- standard procedure used for a research product's appendix of cases or statutes (hard copies provided, PDF files available, hyperlinks provided electronically)
- standard citation used (Bluebook or ALWD)
- expectation to add the work product to a firm database to assist future researchers
- policies on billing clients for research and writing projects
- policies and budgetary limitations regarding electronic research databases
- jurisdictions considered most persuasive if you will be citing precedents outside your own state's jurisdiction

SOME CAUTIONS ABOUT ELECTRONIC RESEARCH

You had unlimited use and full access for subscription databases during law school. Lawyers in private practice rarely have such freedom because of budget constraints and subscription pricing structures. In comparison, government lawyers will often have greater access to databases and fewer restrictions on use.

You need to know your employer's rules for electronic research. Here are some realities about research when you are in practice:

- The contracts that legal employers have with the electronic database providers vary greatly. Your access to electronic research will be at the mercy of that contract. The terms will include charges for actual research time, the list of accessible databases, price differentials among databases, add-on charges for extra usage beyond the contract terms, and much more.
- The size of your firm will often determine which electronic research databases are included within a subscription. Very large firms with multiple offices may be able to negotiate flat-fee contracts allowing for unlimited use of a provider's service. On the other hand, smaller legal employers will often have subscriptions that limit the available databases to specific practice areas and jurisdictions.

- Realize that the electronic research provider that you personally prefer from past research experience may not be one you will have access to at your law firm.
- Some employers will have negotiated a flat rate for unlimited use with one provider but not any other providers. Consequently, you may be able to use the flat-rate database to your heart's content but have to get permission to use the other providers' databases.
- Employer permission to use an electronic research database with unfavorable subscription terms may first require searching in the flat-rate subscription database *and* exhausting all manual resources without success.
- Some employers will prefer that you use free legal databases before you do any electronic research with subscription databases.
- Law librarians at your firm will know the policies on electronic research and can advise you on specific strategies to maximize research dollars.
- The particular research project or the particular client may limit the research sources allowed for a project. A quick, look-see request on the state of the law may not warrant the expense of a subscription database. A client's fee arrangement may also preclude electronic research expenses.
- If you are a new lawyer, keep your legal research and writing textbooks from law school in your desk drawer. If you used relatively few hard-copy resources during law school, you will likely need to review a description of those sources before you head to the library.

The established electronic database providers are coming out with new product versions that are expected in time to replace your current research background. WestlawNext and Lexis Advance are examples of this changing legal research product market.

There may be specialty electronic databases for your practice area that you will not have used previously. Additional databases may include state or federal government resources, specialty updating services, subscription corporate intelligence data, or other products.

Smaller and mid-sized firms will often supplement their own libraries by using courthouse or law school libraries. In addition, employers with fewer dollars for library volumes and subscription research will encourage their lawyers to use free sources on the Internet. More courts throughout the country are posting recent cases on their websites. Many

• •

Examples of Free Legal Research Sites

Google Scholar
http://scholar.google.com

Cornell's Legal Information Institute
www.law.cornell.edu

LexisNexis Communities
www.lexisnesis.com/community/portal/content/lexisone
landingpage.aspx

FindLaw for Legal Professionals
http://lp.findlaw.com

U.S. Government Printing Office's Federal Digital System
(FDsys)
www.gpo.gov/fdsys

THOMAS (Library of Congress)
http://thomas.loc.gov/home/thomas.php

Justia
www.justia.com

Social Science Research Network (SSRN)
www.ssrn.com

New York Law School's DRAGNET
www.nyls.edu/library/research_tools_and_sources/
dragnet1

Source: Elizabeth Caulfield, Head of Reference and Instruction Librarian, Texas Tech
University School of Law

government sites now provide more information online than in the past. See the listing below of some free legal research sources.

THE RESEARCH STEPS ON A PROJECT

As soon as you receive a project, enter the deadline into your personal calendaring system. Set an artificial deadline date at least two days before that actual date and work toward the earlier date. By having two days "buffer" time, you will have extra time if you misplace your flash drive, get writer's block, or encounter a last-minute twist in the research. If you have several projects due on the same day, stagger your artificial deadlines to allow more time: one project two days earlier, one project four days earlier, and so forth.

Determine your current expertise in the practice area of the research. You may need to gain background knowledge before you begin your actual billable research. Firm law librarians can point you to specialty volumes for your jurisdiction that will provide you with background more quickly than a general search. Your background reading will allow you to determine appropriate search terms and plan your research more effectively.

Make sure you are clear on what you are supposed to be researching. Take time to think through everything that your assigning lawyer told you about the project. Consider the following:

- Are you sure you know the specific issue that you are researching? Write out an issue statement to clarify it in your mind.
- What are the specific requirements for the work product you will produce? If you are unfamiliar with the work product format, take the time to learn about that format *before* you begin. Review any firm or document-assembly templates that are relevant to your assignment.
- Are you clear on the time and cost parameters of the assignment? Remind yourself of the time to be expended, the interim and final deadlines, any restrictions on electronic research, and any billing limits.

- Are you aware of the context of the case in which your actual work product will fit? Decide whether you need to ascertain more facts, look at a relevant document, or peruse the letter from opposing counsel that has triggered the research.
- Are you aware of any specific preferences your assigning lawyer has regarding format, style, or other matters?

Plan your research before you start. Think through which sources will be most useful to you. Prioritize the order in which you will move through those sources. Carefully consider your search terms.

If you have multiple issues, keep your materials organized by issue. If necessary, set up a spreadsheet to track the research for each separate issue. Organize case and statute materials for each issue separately. If the same case or statute will be used for several issues, put a copy of it in each issue's organizational stack.

Make sure you keep track of your research as you go along. List every source that you consulted whether or not the search was successful. Also write down search terms used for each source. You may discover a more useful term later in your research and then need to recheck earlier sources using that new search term.

Although tracking is easy with most subscription databases, you will likely use other online and print sources that are not included within those subscription tracking capabilities. You need to have a full account of all sources and terms that you used. It may be more helpful, therefore, to create your own research tracking form. Having all research sources and terms reflected in one place will provide you with a better overview of your project. If your research is completed over a series of days, the form will save you time when reviewing what has already been done and what still needs to be completed. Your research tracking form can be either an electronic or hard-copy version. A sample research tracking form is included below.

• •

Research Tracking Form

Issue:

Assigning Lawyer:

Client File Number:

Deadline:

Resource #1:

_____

_____

Search Terms:

_____

_____

Resource #2:

_____

_____

Search Terms:

_____

_____

Resource #3:

_____

_____

Search Terms:

_____

_____

[Additional resource and search term spaces would be
added as appropriate. Multiple-issue projects would have
entries for each separate issue.]

Periodically pause within the project and evaluate your research findings. Too often researchers will accumulate masses of cases and statutes as if on a treadmill that has no off button. You should regularly stop and review where you are in your research. You do not want to print off additional sources until you fully evaluate what you already have.

Read through the sources that you have collected. Consider the following as you evaluate the status of your research:

- Do you have all the relevant statutes?
- How will the cases impact each party's position (plaintiff or defendant)?
- Are there cases or statutes cited in your current sources that you need to read first before casting your net any wider?
- Have you reached an ending point where you are finding the same sources mentioned and no new sources of significance?
- If not, what search terms and sources do you need to consider next?
- Have you discovered any new, useful search terms so that you now need to recheck prior sources for those same new terms?

Do not rely on headnotes alone during this part of your research. Read every case carefully. Headnotes are written by the editors and are prone to human error. If you depend on the headnote now, you may get wedded to that view in your writing stage and miss the nuances of the actual case.

Alice, a judicial law clerk, was asked by her judge to check all research cited by counsel in their legal memoranda and to complete her own research on the issue as well. In reading the cases cited, it was clear that one lawyer had read only the headnote for the legal proposition he argued and not the full case. The statement of law in the actual judicial opinion was the opposite of the headnote written by the reporter's editor. Alice indicated the lawyer's error in interpretation in her memo to the judge. The lawyer was embarrassed when the judge pointed out his error in front of his client and opposing counsel.

Organize your research materials in stages throughout the project. In addition to evaluating your research findings periodically to see where you are in the process, you will want to organize your research in order to make the later writing process easier. By doing so, you will be less likely to overlook gaps in your research before you begin the writing process.

Stop at various points throughout your research to summarize each of the relevant statutes and brief each of the cases that you have found. Turn any sections that you have highlighted in cases into actual notes rather than retaining them as mere highlights. This process will force you to think more deeply about the source rather than keeping it in a more nebulous "probably or possibly useful" category.

Make an outline of what you have found in your research. Include three levels in your outline: topics, subtopics, and supporting points. Then indicate the cases and statutes that you tentatively plan to use for each level. Next to each source, place a short comment to indicate how you may use that source. The comment might read "definition of element one," "supports plaintiff's position on element three," "policy argument for defendant," or "seminal case still being followed."

You will realize where you have holes in your outline and need to look for additional sources. You will see where you have multiple sources for the same proposition. You may also discover that you have completed one area of the research and need to move on to the next area.

If you get stumped during your legal research, get assistance. Ask the librarians for suggestions on additional sources or search terms to pursue. They can direct you to other electronic resources, request items for you through interlibrary loan, and advise you on available resources in the library collections at area courthouses or law schools.

Helplines and Internet assistance are available for many database providers. However, determine whether such assistance is included in your firm's subscription or if there will be an add-on charge. Be very careful when using non-firm assistance that you do not unintentionally breach client confidentiality by divulging sensitive information about the issues you are researching.

If you come across a side issue to the research that could potentially be important, ask whether you need to pursue it. Do not make an assumption that the side issue can be ignored. If the lawyer says no when you query the need to research the side issue, then you are covered. However, if the lawyer would have said yes and you did not ask, your finished product will be incomplete and may even be wrong. It is extremely hard to re-create a research thread if later discussions with the assigning lawyer reveal that you must go back and complete the research you initially ignored.

Do not forget to update your sources. With electronic updating, there is no excuse for not checking subsequent history. However, even if you must check for updates manually, just grit your teeth and do it. If relevant to your assignment, you also want to explore whether any bills in the current legislative session will affect your research. A footnote regarding potential amendments or repeal of relevant statutes will alert your assigning lawyer to possible changes in the law.

If you are using a law librarian for assistance in accessing cases, make sure you know the firm's policy on updating. The policy may be that law librarians only check subsequent history if specifically asked to do so. Make known any updating requirements you have.

ORGANIZING YOUR WRITING PROJECT

If you have organized your sources in stages throughout your research, it will be easier to complete your final organization to begin writing. Careful organization is important if you are going to achieve the most professional work product.

Realize that prewriting is an important stage in the writing process. The thought process after your research is complete and before you put words on the page is critical to the final product. Professional writers recognize that the steps before they begin writing, when they mull over ideas and organize for the actual writing, are essential preparation for an excellent final product. Allow yourself time for this stage rather than rushing to begin writing immediately.

Take time again to review each of your statute summaries and case briefs as well as the full-text sources. Carefully reevaluate what you have before you go any further. Ask yourself these questions:

- Did you miss anything important on your initial reading and briefing of cases or summarizing of statutes?
- Do you still take the same position on how the source will impact each party's arguments?
- Does the source fit into another section of your outline better than where you originally indicated?
- Does the source need to be referenced in more than one section of your work product?
- Are there any statutes, cases, or other legal authorities cited in a source that you still need to read?
- Did you update every source for subsequent history?
- Did you carefully follow up on any items that the subsequent history indicated might increase or decrease the authority's persuasiveness?

Look at the outline that you made throughout the research project. Evaluate it carefully before you go any further on the project.

- Have you included in your outline all the topics, subtopics, and supporting points that are needed?
- Does anything need to be moved within the outline because it logically belongs in a different place than where you initially thought you would discuss it?
- Are there any points within the outline that you now understand at the end of your research are not important to the analysis and can be removed?
- Do you have any gaps in the outline that indicate you need to complete additional research on those points?

Choose which section of your work product to write first. You may not write the sections in the order that they will appear in the final document. For example, in a memorandum, you may want to leave the brief answer and the conclusion until last. You may find the statement of facts to be the best starting point and then follow with the questions presented. For a client letter, you may prefer to summarize all factual background information before laying out the relevant law.

Rather than attempt to write the perfect draft, just start writing. Get the words on paper and then polish your work. Few people can write perfect sentences and paragraphs initially. Trying to craft each sentence as it goes on paper is likely to stall your thought process and actually delay your writing progress.

If you should encounter writer's block, just begin writing anything. It might be unconnected thoughts and have nothing to do with your final document, but the key is to start writing. You can always discard the initial drivel later, but you need to get words on paper and break through the writing block.

Plan to spend approximately 80 percent of your writing time on revisions after your initial draft. Professional writers spend most of their time on revisions. The first draft of your document is likely to be merely acceptable, or at best good. You want to turn out your very best work product rather than a first draft. Allow yourself time for multiple careful revisions. Law firms pay you for excellent work, and clients demand it.

Regain your context if you get interrupted in your writing. Even with dedicated blocks of project time in your schedule, you are likely to need multiple days to complete an assignment. You will usually write in stages amid client interviews, meetings, or other assignments you are working on simultaneously. Whenever you have to stop writing, make careful notes regarding the next task to complete and your train of thought before the interruption. You can make the notes directly in the text in a different font, underlined, or highlighted. Or if you prefer, make the comments on a sticky note in your research file.

When you come back to your writing after a delay, take the time to reread the last section you wrote in order to get your context back. You are much less likely to be repetitive or to miss a connection in your analysis if you spend this time. Your quick notes when you stopped will help, but they will not give you the same mindset as rereading the section again.

If you have initially written segments of your document in an order different from the final structure, read the sections in the correct order and rewrite as necessary to form an integrated whole. Consider when you first introduced information within the document and decide whether it should be introduced earlier or referenced later. Check for consistency throughout the entire document. Add transitions to create a more readable flow among the sections. Decide whether your reader can easily follow your analysis throughout the entire document.

Allow sufficient time for editing in multiple stages. Editing is time consuming because you must check carefully the many detailed layers within a written project. If you try to edit once for everything within the document, you will miss specific errors—but your reader will notice all those you missed. You will want to do multiple edits, focusing on one specific aspect during each edit.

The following list includes some of the separate editing steps you will need time for:

- statutory language and interpretation
- correct case information (facts, reasoning, and holdings) and analysis
- the logic of your analysis in each section
- transition between sections
- the overall logic and consistency throughout the entire document
- clarity and readability
- wordiness and repetition
- grammar, punctuation, spelling, and typographical errors
- correct quotations
- correct citations
- format problems
- footnotes or endnotes
- tables, exhibits, and appendixes

What should you do if you encounter problems and are delayed in your project? If you are concerned that you are not going to be able to make a deadline as promised, it is best to alert the assigning lawyer as soon as possible and negotiate a reasonable extension. Make sure you are able to explain the reasons for the delay succinctly. If asked how long you need, give a new deadline that you can actually meet—do not underestimate because of embarrassment.

PRESENTING YOUR RESEARCH ORALLY INSTEAD OF IN WRITING

Do not make the mistake of thinking you can prepare less for an oral report on your research than for a written work product. Many of the tips in the prior section on organizing your writing will also prepare you for an oral presentation. For an oral presentation, consider the following:

- Evaluate each source carefully.
- Make an outline for your oral presentation.
- Include specific notes on any complex aspects.
- Consider questions you may be asked and prepare your answers.
- Practice your presentation aloud multiple times.

PRESENTING YOUR RESEARCH IN AN E-MAIL

Because e-mail has become so accepted in business communications, you may be asked to present your research results in an e-mail to your assigning lawyer or client instead of in a more traditional format.[1] An e-mail format will require you to become an expert at conciseness while not losing any of the precise analysis. Keep the following points in mind:

- Keep the communication formal and professional and do not degenerate into informality because of the social uses of e-mail.
- Use headings, subheadings, bulleted lists, numbered lists, and indentations to facilitate easier reading.

---

1. E-mail presentation of research may require your e-mail text to stand alone or may consider the e-mail text to summarize the attachment of a full-length legal memorandum. You need to know which format is expected and tailor your presentation accordingly.

- Carefully craft each sentence and paragraph and intentionally select your word choices.
- Edit in separate stages for each aspect of the document: logic of the analysis; readability; transition between sections; sentence structure; grammar, punctuation, and spelling; citation.
- Reread the entire e-mail before you hit "send" to make sure it is clear, complete, and professional.

Even if you have been asked to research a very narrow question and to summarize your research in an e-mail, you will still want to have thorough documentation of your research in your files in case a question arises later. Be sure to include in your files complete notes on your research findings, an outline of your findings as though a memo were required, copies of all the cases and statutes, and your research tracking form. If the research project was extensive, you may want to ask your assigning lawyer if a legal memorandum would be helpful as a follow-up step to the e-mail summary that you provided. In any event, retain the same documentation for your files as you would for a shorter e-mail research assignment.

AFTER THE PROJECT IS COMPLETED

Most assigning lawyers will not initiate a follow-up meeting to give you feedback on the work you completed. However, you want feedback so you can improve your work—especially if you have completed your first project for a lawyer and want to excel on future assignments.

After the project has been reviewed, ask whether the assigning lawyer would be willing to meet with you to provide constructive feedback so you can improve your next work product for the lawyer. Some assigning lawyers will not have the time or the inclination to meet with you, but those who do will be providing you with valuable assistance. By taking the initiative to ask for feedback and showing maturity in your acceptance of constructive criticism, you will indicate that your personal work standard is excellence and that you respect the lawyer's advice.

Reflection and Strategies

1. Which types of legal research do you feel most proficient at and why? Least proficient and why? What strategies for improvement could you implement?
2. Which types of writing projects do you feel most proficient at and why? Least proficient and why? What strategies for improvement could you implement?
3. What are your strengths and weaknesses in planning and organizing your research projects? Consider strategies to capitalize on the strengths and to ameliorate the weaknesses.
4. What are your strengths and weaknesses in planning and organizing your writing projects? Consider strategies to capitalize on the strengths and to ameliorate the weaknesses.
5. What are your major areas of difficulty among the editing tasks, and how can you improve your editing skills?
6. What differences in requirements have you noticed among the supervisors for whom you complete research and writing projects?

Telephones, E-mail, and Social Media

Technology has drastically changed the practice of law. A constant stream of new e-mail messages flows into inboxes throughout the day. Smartphones make us accessible 24/7 by text, e-mail, and telephone. We fear that everyone expects attention NOW and immediate responses regardless of how important or trivial the communication is.

The technological impact on our lives has become so extensive that some psychologists specialize in treating Internet and smartphone addictions. Although technology is useful, we need to be very aware that it can interrupt our work, waste our time, and lure us into burnout. Your time and work management skills can help you effectively juggle your projects and tasks as well as the many electronic demands on your day.

GETTING THE MOST OUT OF TELEPHONE CALLS

Two aspects are important to positive telephone communication. First, you want to avoid any misunderstandings, hurt feelings, or bad impressions. Second, you want the conversations to be completed with the desired results in the least amount of time.

Long-standing etiquette rules exist for business telephone conversations. However, many lawyers have developed informal habits through texting and e-mailing friends and may overlook these rules. Some business etiquette basics to remember include the following:

- Decide whether a telephone call is the best way to deliver the particular news or information that you must communicate.
  - A meeting is more appropriate in situations requiring lengthy discussions, give-and-take negotiations, the delivery of bad news, the discussion of disputed topics, or the building of trust in a client relationship.
  - Although telephone calls provide tone of voice and inflection as cues, they can still be easily misunderstood because they lack

the cues of body language, gestures, and facial expressions that are present in meetings.

* You will spend more time making amends for a misunderstood telephone conversation than you would have initially spent in a meeting.

- If at all possible, do not take telephone calls while you have someone in your office for an appointment or meeting. The person you are with should be your priority and have your undivided attention.

- If you know that an important call is expected and may interrupt the meeting at some point, inform the person in your office that this may occur and apologize up front that there may be an interruption.

- If you must take an unexpected, important call while someone is in your office, apologize for the interruption before you answer the telephone.

- Remember confidentiality. If you receive a call when another person is present, decide whether the call is one that should not be overheard. If so, ask the person in your office to wait in the reception area.

- Always identify yourself when you answer the telephone. Your employer may have a preferred format for you to use. If not, state your first and last name and say, "How may I help you?" This is much more polite than merely stating your name.

- Answer the telephone call with enthusiasm. You want the person on the other end to respond to your energy and confidence. An old-fashioned adage of telephone etiquette states, "Smile when you answer the telephone."

- If someone calls and you have limited time to talk, diplomatically state a time limit for the call. "I only have ten minutes before a meeting. Will that be enough time, or do you want to schedule a later time for me to return your call?"

- If a telephone conversation goes beyond the time you have indicated, politely bring it to a close. "Unfortunately, I must go to my meeting now and will have to end our call. I'll be happy to look at the document and call you back tomorrow morning."

- If the other party gets off topic, try to redirect the call back to the topic or move the conversation forward. "So the first thing I need to do for you is _____, and the second thing is _____. Was there a third item I need to complete?"

Most of these basic etiquette rules focus on telephone calls that you received and answered yourself. There are two additional categories of telephone calls you need to consider: the telephone calls you initiate and the telephone calls you return. Although you will handle each type of telephone call as having the same level of importance, you do want to consider them somewhat differently.

For the telephone calls you initiate:

Choose carefully the times at which you make your own calls. Initiate telephone calls at times that are good for your workload so you can focus on the conversation without interruptions. Make telephone calls first thing in the morning if that is a quieter time in your office. By completing telephone calls early, you can gather information needed for any projects later in the day. By having a second time in the afternoon when you initiate telephone calls, you can resolve any questions or concerns that have surfaced during your workday.

Prioritize your telephone calls. Determine the order for your telephone calls. In addition to the importance of the matter, consider whether your client will be available at that time, whether you have enough time in your schedule to complete the call without rushing, and whether the information from the call might impact other tasks you need to complete during the day.

Plan your telephone conversation before you place the call. You will complete the telephone call in less time if you have carefully considered the outcome you want, the important points you want to make, and how you want to communicate each point. Make some notes to guide the conversation if you need to do so. Consider questions that the other party might ask and prepare your answers.

Be aware of any confidentiality concerns and client preferences regarding messages. Discuss with your client early on in the relationship with whom you may leave messages and whether you may leave detailed messages on voicemail or an answering machine. One client may prefer that you leave only your name and telephone number; another may be comfortable with your leaving detailed messages with only one specific person.

Before you place the call, consider the appropriate message to leave if the person is unavailable. By doing so, you are more likely to remember your client's preferences and have a message composed that meets those parameters. You are also more likely to include everything in the message rather than rambling or forgetting a point.

If you need to leave a message, be brief but thorough. Enunciate so that the message will not be lost in mumbled words. Assuming that you have no confidentiality concerns about leaving the message, you should:

- Identify yourself and give your telephone number.
- State specifically your reasons for the telephone call. If it is to give information, state the message precisely. If it is to get information, list the specific questions that you need to have answered.
- If there are convenient times for the person to return your call, state that information.
- If you want the person to leave the information on your voicemail or with your assistant should you be unavailable for the return call, indicate that preference.
- End the call with your name and telephone number a second time.

Keep in touch with your clients. Perhaps the cardinal rule in communication is to contact your clients with periodic updates rather than have them chase you for an update on a legal matter. Consider the following points:

- Whether a face-to-face meeting, letter, telephone call, or e-mail is most appropriate will depend on the information you have to communicate.
- Even if you can only report that you are still waiting for additional information or that things are on course, let your client know that much.
- One of the most common complaints from unsatisfied clients is difficulty in getting any information from their lawyers.
- Lawyers who do not communicate may lose a client for the firm, need to respond to a partner who has received a complaint, or even end up with a disciplinary investigation by the state bar.

For the telephone calls you return:

Find the balance between being responsive and getting your work done. You want to give your clients personalized service and be available to them. However, you also want to finish work for all clients in a timely manner. Set reasonable boundaries on your availability. Whether you resort to voicemail taking your messages, an answering service handling your telephone calls, or a staff member fielding client inquiries, you need to minimize interruptions temporarily when you are focusing on projects.

Know your employer's procedures and policies. You want to make sure that you know your employer's guidelines for handling telephone calls. Even though employers are concerned about client care, most of them realize that lawyers cannot always be available because of projects, court appearances, and client meetings. Most clients are reasonable people who are not offended with leaving a message when you are unavailable. If necessary, clear any change in your routine for answering your telephone calls with your supervisor.

Allow a staff member to field your calls when you are working on a project that needs concentration. If you are fortunate enough to have an assigned staff member, use that person to monitor your telephone calls. Implement several steps so that your clients will not feel slighted and will be pleased with the service they receive:

- Whenever possible, introduce your clients to the staff member who takes messages for you. The client and staff member will both have a face to go with the name. Let your client know that the staff member has your full confidence and will handle any matters professionally.
- Tell your staff member the people whose calls you will *always* take, even if they call during your quiet time for projects: partners, clients, court clerks, family members, or others. Keep the list to a reasonable length so that it does not become almost everyone.
- Tell your staff member the people whose calls you will take *temporarily* for the day because you have been playing telephone tag or need information from them as soon as possible.
- If your staff member knows your client base and has sound judgment, allow some discretion for interrupting you with a telephone call if it seems appropriately important.
- Designate at least three times during the day when you will always return telephone messages that have accumulated during your project time. Choosing mid-morning, mid-afternoon, and before the close of business as the times will allow you to return most calls within roughly two or three hours of when the message was left.
- Have your staff member capture in a telephone message all the details that are necessary for your particular practice. The following generic information would typically be needed unless you know the caller already:
  - the date of the call
  - the time of the call
  - the person's name
  - the person's contact numbers: business, home, cell (and preference for use to return the call)
  - the person's company or business
  - the person's reason for calling
  - any materials that you need in front of you when returning the call

- other information that may be relevant: referral by another lawyer, friend of one of your clients, opposing counsel for a matter
- the time period when the person needs you to return the call (if different from the time periods when you always return calls)

Alternatively, allow your voicemail to take messages while you are working on projects. Make sure that your voicemail message is professional and sounds genuinely interested in speaking with the caller. Your message should:

- include a clear identification of whose voicemail has been reached
- leave brief instructions for the caller rather than a long message, but include any specific information you would like them to leave in the message
- caution the caller against leaving confidential information on your voicemail
- ask the caller to repeat the name and telephone number twice, preferably at both the beginning and the end of the message; hopefully, one of the versions will be completely understandable

Always return phone calls—always. It is tempting not to return a telephone call when you do not have anything new to report to a client. However, you do not want to risk hard feelings on the part of the client because you ignored a message. Even if you have nothing to report, take the short time to call and say exactly that. Try to return telephone calls within two or three hours if at all possible, but by the end of the day is essential. If you cannot do so personally, then have your staff member return the call so the client will not feel ignored. You can follow up the next day if the staff member was unable to handle the client's concern.

Always leave a message when you return a call and miss the person. You want the client to know that you attempted to respond. If appropriate, tell the client when you will call again or when it would be most convenient for a client callback. Make a note for yourself of the

day/time you returned the telephone call in case you need later verification. If you are unable to reach a person after several attempts, consider
e-mailing to say that you have been unsuccessful in reaching the person
by telephone and to please contact you again.

Short-circuit the game of telephone tag. When you and a caller
seem to never connect, consider the following possibilities to resolve the
matter:

- If you initiated a call and missed the return call, leave a message
  asking the person to answer the specific question you have or provide you with the specific information you need. Indicate that it
  is fine to leave that response on your voicemail or with your staff
  member. If your staff member will be fielding the return call, make
  sure that staff member knows the specific questions to ask or the
  information needed.
- If you think the caller is merely after information or a response to
  an earlier query, leave the information in your telephone message
  and ask them to call you if they need anything additional.
- If a discussion with the person is essential, suggest a telephone
  appointment time so that you can both be available to talk. The
  time can be specific for your calendar: "I'll pencil you in for a
  telephone conference tomorrow at 9:00 a.m." You can also suggest a range of time on your calendar: "I'll be available between
  3:00 and 4:30 p.m. this afternoon." Make sure it is clear who will
  initiate the telephone call at the indicated time.

THE SMARTPHONE AS AN EXTENSION OF THE OFFICE

Whether you own a BlackBerry, iPhone, Droid, or some other smartphone, the technology has altered the way lawyers work. Big Law
employers pay you the high salary with the expectation that you will
earn your money by responding to clients and to them any time you
are needed. Life's new rule is to check your smartphone regularly for
messages.

The Internet is at your fingertips, and the array of apps available is
astonishing. Lawyers are taking advantage of apps for everything from

the Federal Rules of Civil Procedure and *Black's Law Dictionary* to counting days for deadlines and editing Word documents. There are several informative, law-related blogs dealing with smartphones.

• •

Law-Related Blogs Dealing with Smartphones

iPhone J.D.: Lawyers using iPhones and iPads
www.iphonejd.com

The Droid Lawyer
http://thedroidlawyer.com

Be aware of business etiquette for smartphones. Many lawyers have grown up with cell phones, e-mail, and texting as part of their lives. Consequently, they are not always aware that different etiquette rules apply in the professional workplace than with friends and family. Here is some smartphone business etiquette to remember:

- When texting on business matters, leave out the cutesy text acronyms, such as LOL and OMG, and any emoticons.
- Put your smartphone away when you are sitting in a meeting, talking with a client, sitting in court, or discussing a matter with another lawyer. It is rude to be looking at your phone constantly in these circumstances. Clients will not be pleased that you are more interested in another client or personal matters than in them.
- In these same circumstances, do not secretively check your smartphone or send a text under the table. You are not fooling anyone. It is still rude.
- Even in the very rare instance when you are with a client and legitimately checking an e-mail or app on your smartphone because it is pertinent to the discussion, remain very client focused. Do not fixate on the screen and continue to tap in commands while talking

to the client. Retain eye contact with the client as you discuss what is on the screen.

- Silence your smartphone when you are sitting in a meeting, talking with a client, sitting in court, or discussing a matter with another lawyer. It is rude to have your ringtone interrupt business events. Unless your smartphone has a very quiet vibrate setting, the interruption can still be rude.
- Choose a ringtone appropriate for a professional environment. No matter how popular the song is with your peers, it will not impress your partners or clients.
- In court, always be on your best behavior with your smartphone. The consequences can be embarrassing or worse if you misuse your technology.
- Remember not to take or make personal calls when you are in professional settings. Your client will not be amused if you spend the time during a court recess telephoning to make a dinner date with a woman you met at the gym.

Smartphones have become an integral part of most lawyers' lives. However, they can become a major distractor in their personal lives and lead to what some refer to as smartphone addiction.

For a look at BlackBerry addiction, read *CrackBerry: True Tales of BlackBerry Use and Abuse* by Gary Mazo, Martin Trautschold, and Kevin Michaluk (Apress 2010).

USING E-MAIL MORE EFFECTIVELY

Electronic mail was seen as a great triumph when it was first introduced because it is a convenient and fast way to handle a large number of matters. Unless e-mails are carefully drafted and presented in a readable style, however, they can cause misunderstandings. You need to become adept at effective and efficient e-mail communications.

For many people, using e-mail is stressful because of the enormous volume of e-mails received and the perceived pressure for instant responses. You need to organize your e-mails to avoid becoming over-whelmed by the sheer number.

Studies have documented the negative impact of e-mail on productivity in the workplace because employees lose focus with the repeated interruptions during their completion of important tasks. Unless you manage e-mail effectively, you will risk being distracted by it and getting less done as a result.

Consider these tips for diminishing e-mail interruptions during your workday. You want to prevent e-mails from constantly distracting you when you need to stay focused on a project. A number of strategies exist for minimizing e-mail interruptions:

- Set aside particular blocks of time when you will not look at e-mails.
  - Ideally, just check your e-mail at set times *after* your regularly scheduled project time.[1]
  - If that is not possible, check your e-mail only every half hour or hour.
  - Handle only the urgent e-mails before you go back to your project; do not get distracted by other, nonurgent e-mails.
- If you have a staff member assigned to you, direct some clients to send e-mails to that staff member rather than to your own e-mail account.
  - The staff member can monitor those e-mails and forward the ones to you that you need to handle personally.
  - If using this method, make sure you introduce your staff member to the clients and let them know that you have complete confidence in that person.
- Minimize distractions from the general e-mail alert sound and the new item alert window.

---

1. See Chapter 4 for information about scheduling regular blocks of project time during your week.

- Lower the volume for the alert sound and shorten the time that the alert window is on the screen to reduce the intensity of e-mail distractions.
- Minimize your inbox screen so that you are not constantly distracted by the incoming messages.
- Use the rules tool to select alert sounds and alert windows for e-mails from only a few specific individuals (your supervisor, a major client, the managing partner, or others appropriate to your circumstances) rather than for all e-mails. You can change the rules easily to add or delete people to the list.
- Turn the alert and pop-up off temporarily while you are working on a project.

- Create a rule to move new e-mails from listserv and other subscription services that are useful but not critical directly to inbox folders rather appearing within your main inbox.
  - Have each subscription's inbox folder clearly labeled: "Ag Law listserv," "State Bar Newsletter," "State Ag E-journal."
  - Read the items in these inbox folders daily, weekly, or less often as appropriate to the particular source.
- Create a rule for moving e-mails to inbox folders also for any outside community organizations or bar associations for which you hold board, committee, or officer positions.
- Use the Really Simple Syndication (RSS) tool to get legal headline feeds from websites that interest you. Create a rule so that these e-mails go to individual RSS folders instead of directly into your main inbox.

Tips for choosing when e-mail is appropriate for the task. E-mail is not always the best means of communication.

- Decide whether an e-mail message is the best way to deliver the particular news or information that you must communicate.
  - A meeting is more appropriate in situations requiring lengthy discussions, give-and-take negotiations, the delivery of bad

news, the discussion of disputed topics, or the building of trust in a new client relationship.

- E-mails can be easily misunderstood because they lack the cues that are present in meetings: body language, gestures, facial expressions, tone of voice, and inflection.
- You will spend more time making amends for a misunderstood e-mail message than you would have initially spent in a meeting.

- Decide whether an e-mail can accomplish the task efficiently and effectively.
  - People often waste an enormous amount of time responding to multiple e-mails when they could have accomplished the same task more efficiently and effectively in person.
  - A meeting is more efficient and effective when you need extensive discussion, generation of ideas, input from multiple people, or agreement from a group with divergent views.
  - If the group is geographically scattered, use videoconferencing or some other meeting alternative.
- Decide whether the information is needed *right now*. If not, use an internal memo or note rather than an e-mail message.
- Decide which people *really* need to receive the e-mail, and do not send or copy the e-mail to anyone else.
- Ask yourself whether using an e-mail could lead to any ethical or other problems:
  - an unintended lawyer-client relationship
  - loss of attorney-client privilege
  - conflict-of-interest problems
  - confidential information being divulged

Consider these tips for writing e-mails that are more effective.
E-mails need the same care as other modes of written communication.

- Remember that you are writing a formal communication and not an informal message to family or friends.
  - Use complete sentences and paragraphs.

- Always use proper grammar and punctuation. Do not depend on the grammar and punctuation tools built into your software; they are often wrong.
- Always check your spelling. Do not depend on spell-check to catch everything; it will not catch correctly spelled words that are used in the wrong context.
- Watch out for any typographical errors.

- Organize your thoughts *before* you write. You want your e-mail to be logical and complete rather than disorganized.

- Use concise sentences with carefully chosen words, and keep paragraphs short. Delete flowery language, complex clauses, vague phrases, and imprecise words.

- Carefully reread your entire e-mail before sending it to determine if every statement is totally clear, if you have accomplished exactly what you intended, and if the e-mail is polite and professional.

- Remember that e-mails are most effective when they are one screen or shorter in length. However, realize that smartphone recipients tend to scan without as much care as recipients who read the e-mail on their full-sized computer screens.

- If you must send an e-mail longer than one screen, attach a document that can include all the details you want in the communication. Summarize the document in your e-mail and request that readers review the entire document in detail.

- Always include a subject line for your e-mail to help your recipient determine which e-mails to read first among the hundreds received. Include enough important information for the recipient to understand immediately what the content will be. "Contract" is unhelpful, whereas "Draft contract for sale of Anderson Brothers" will assist your recipient.

- When you need the recipient to complete a task or respond, put your request and any deadline at the beginning of the e-mail: "Please reply to points 3 and 4 by 5:00 p.m. on Monday, March 3." Also consider indicating the request or deadline in the e-mail subject line: "RE: ABC, Inc., Draft Contract; Reply needed by 5:00 p.m. on 3/3."

- Remind your recipient in the text of your e-mail of any context for the message: "opposing counsel has requested" or "per item 6 in Rodney Smith's memo" or "under the local rules of the Madison County Court."
- Use headings, subheadings, bulleted lists, or numbered lists to organize your e-mail for easier reading.
- Limit attachments to only the important ones and title each attachment file so that the reader knows exactly what it contains. "Johnson Affidavit.doc" is more helpful than "Johnson1.doc."
- Remember to attach the appropriate files. If you forget, you will have to write a second e-mail sending the attachment, or the recipient will have to send an e-mail asking for the missing item.
- Determine whether you need to designate the message as high importance so that the recipient will respond quickly. Use this designation only if the e-mail is indeed urgent.
- Add a standard signature block to your e-mail with name, title, firm, address, telephone number, e-mail address, fax number, website, or other details.
- Because e-mails are occasionally misdirected, include the firm's standard disclaimer at the bottom of all e-mails being sent outside the firm. To avoid sending the e-mail to the wrong person, always check the recipients and their e-mail addresses carefully.
- Avoid the back-and-forth "thank you" and "you're welcome" e-mails unless you need to confirm that you received the initial e-mail.

Avoid these absolute no-no's for business e-mail. There are some rules that should never be broken when using e-mail.

- Do not accidentally hit "reply all" on a group e-mail when only the sender needs to know your response. The other people do not need any unnecessary e-mails. If your reply was meant to be private for just the sender, you may inadvertently divulge information that you did not want others to know.

- Do not include text acronyms in an e-mail: BTW, LOL, OMG, IMHO. Your message may not be understandable to recipients who do not text regularly. Also do not use emoticons. These items will make you look unprofessional.
- Do not use all capital letters, which is the equivalent of yelling at the recipient. Instead use bold, italics, or underlining to draw attention to a point or a deadline.
- Never hit "send" when you have typed an e-mail filled with mean remarks, catty observations, accusations of blame, or other negative comments. Reread the e-mail later when you are no longer angry—and then delete it. You will regret sending an angry e-mail and will not be able to undo the damage.
- Avoid using your business e-mail account to send and receive personal e-mails. Employers diligently state their e-mail policies and will argue that there is no privacy expectation. You do not want your employer to find out information you would prefer not to be known.
- Along those lines, do not apply for new jobs with other employers using your business e-mail account. Your own employer may find out during a review of employee e-mail accounts. The potential employer will frown on your unprofessional use of your current employer's e-mail.
- Do not send anything by e-mail that you do not want Auntie Em, Granny Smith, and the rest of the world to see. Your embarrassing e-mail will be forwarded to the entire firm and then on to everyone's e-mail contacts. It will likely surface on at least one legal blog as well.

Consider these tips for efficient handling of your inbox e-mails. Organization in sorting and responding to the e-mails in your inbox is essential to good work management.

- Look for and respond first to any e-mails designated high importance or with subject headings that you know are important matters.

- Set your e-mail options so an alert will appear if you are not looking at the last e-mail in a conversation thread.
- If possible, determine what to do with an e-mail the first time you read it:
  - **Reply to it.** Send an answer immediately if the e-mail does not require a long reply. Reply to all e-mails within twenty-four hours even if you merely reply, "I'll get back to you on this matter."
  - **Forward it.** If you do not need the e-mail but the information would benefit someone else, forward it with a comment as to why you are doing so.
  - **Delegate it.** If the e-mail contains a task you need to assign to someone else, forward it with instructions.
    - If appropriate, change the subject line when you forward the message.
    - Flag your copy of the e-mail for follow-up with the staff member on the relevant date.
  - **File it.** Assign the e-mail to a relevant inbox archive folder if it needs to be kept after you have read it. Alternatively, file it in an electronic client file or print it for filing in a hard-copy file.
  - **Delete it.** Whenever possible, delete e-mails as soon as they are read or handled.
- Use the "block sender" designation for any junk e-mail that gets past your spam filters. The e-mail will be removed to junk e-mail immediately and in the future.
- Unsubscribe from any legitimate e-mail distribution list in which you are no longer interested.
- In addition to times when you regularly check your e-mail throughout the day, take five minutes in the morning, mid-afternoon, and late afternoon to review your inbox in case you overlooked any items.
- On Friday afternoon, spend a few minutes completing any matters still outstanding for your inbox: responding, sorting, filing, deleting.

- Use the tools for your e-mail system (sort, rules, flags, categories, filters, and others) to help you manage your inbox.

Consider these tips for using archive folders for e-mail storage. An organized archiving system promotes faster retrieval of e-mails when you need them later.

- If available for your e-mail system, set up archived file folders on another storage drive rather than within your inbox. Then archived folders will not count against your mailbox space quota.
- Use a consistent naming system for your e-mail folders and subfolders.
- Use subfolders within a folder to sort e-mails more specifically. If you are on the firm's marketing committee, the folder might be "Marketing" with subfolders for "Meetings," "Brochure Copy," and "Website."
- Where subfolders in different folders have similar names, differentiate the names to indicate the correct folder. If you have a subfolder for meetings in both the marketing committee and the technology committee folders, label the subfolders "M Meetings" and "T Meetings" for easy differentiation.
- Ask the following questions before you decide to store an e-mail in any folder or subfolder:
  - Do I really need to keep this e-mail?
  - Can I keep just the last e-mail in the conversation thread and eliminate the earlier e-mails?
  - Will someone else have this e-mail if I delete it and need it later?
  - Should I add this e-mail to an electronic or hard-copy client file rather than keep it in an archive folder?
  - Should I add a hard copy of this e-mail to my reference desk folders or my tickler file rather than keep an electronic copy?[2]

---

2. See Chapter 4 for more information on reference desk folders and the tickler file system.

- Realize that any auto-archive option will move older items from your inbox to a separate archived inbox. You do not want to forget the items that have been moved.
  - You may be able to schedule the auto-archive function to occur after a specific number of days. However, your law firm's system may override the auto-archive settings with firm-wide settings.
  - If you intentionally hold items in your inbox for long periods of time, you want to turn off this option if the settings do not match the time period that you need.
  - To avoid not knowing when archiving has occurred, have the auto-archive tool prompt you before it completes the action.
- At least once a month, schedule time to go through your file folders and subfolders to delete e-mails that are no longer needed.

SOCIAL MEDIA: MOVING WITH THE TIMES WITHOUT GETTING TRIPPED UP

Google+, Facebook, LinkedIn, Twitter, YouTube, and blogs are just some of the social media and networking tools that lawyers are using in addition to their official firm websites. These technology tools can be used effectively to communicate with other lawyers, find out information about opposing counsel, keep tabs on an opposing party's behavior, vet a prospective employee, and learn more about prospective clients. Social media can also generate client contacts from those who read your blog postings or your comments on blogs and follow your tweets.

These new technologies have moved business development and marketing for lawyers into somewhat unpredictable territory. Professional rules of conduct apply in these new situations, but lawyers and state bar associations do not always agree on how the professional rules should be interpreted.

State bars have issued legal ethics opinions to try to deal with the questions raised. The American Bar Association appointed the Commission on Ethics 20/20 to review the professional rules and draft proposed changes to reflect technological developments. In August 2012, the ABA House of Delegates adopted several of the proposed rules. Lawyers can expect the professional rules to evolve in the coming years as further advances in technology occur and new questions are raised about ethical uses of technology.

Many of the tips that are pertinent to good telephone or e-mail manners would translate over to this area as well. However, a few additional things need to be mentioned:

- Make sure you are aware of any employer policies regarding use of social media. Remember that your employer may monitor social media.

- Realize that social media's usual informality does not apply to you as a lawyer. Be careful about the information you include about yourself and your lifestyle in your profiles and postings; always keep it very professional.

- Understand the intricacies of the privacy settings for each social media site and stay up to date on any changes that occur; do not assume anything about the privacy of your communications, as most social media sites are only peripherally concerned with users' privacy interests.

- Be careful about whom you choose to have as "friends," "fans," and "followers." Stories abound about lawyers and judges who used poor judgment in their choices and their subsequent postings and tweets.

- Use available applications to manage "friends," "fans," and "followers" lists as the number of contacts grows.

- Be vigilant about confidentiality, attorney-client privilege, potential lawyer-client relationships, and potential conflicts of interest. Post appropriate disclaimers to avoid these issues.

- Avoid posting anything that refers to your present or past cases. Opposing parties, your client's corporate competitors, or members of the news media may combine what you thought was an innocent reference with other public information to identify a specific client or court case.

- Monitor comments posted to your blog for inappropriate content, spam, or violations of your state bar's advertising and other rules. If available, use the function that allows you to review all comments, and choose the ones to post rather than accepting all comments for posting automatically. Monitor responses to your tweets for the same reasons.

- Be careful that you do not respond publicly (the "reply all" equivalent in e-mail) when you meant to comment to just one person. Remember that even if you respond privately to someone, that person may decide to disseminate your comments more broadly.
- Recognize that once something is on social media, it will likely be there for posterity and everyone will see it. Tools for removing information after the fact depend on the social media used. They are at best slow in getting results and often nonexistent or unreliable.
- Talk to your staff members about appropriate use of social media. They might think they are just commenting about their interesting or stressful day without realizing the implications of what they say about a client, a lawyer, or the firm.
- Talk with your clients about appropriate use of social media as well. Their comments on social media can divulge a negotiation strategy you discussed or destroy the positive image you were trying to portray of them.

Technology offers many benefits in the fast-paced legal environment. Embrace the time-saving aspects while being well aware of the mishaps that can occur for the unwary user.

....

Reflection and Strategies

1. What rules of business etiquette for the telephone do you need to adopt that are different from your current techniques?
2. For your employment situation, is it more efficient and effective to use voicemail, an answering machine, an

answering service, or a staff member to field telephone calls when you need uninterrupted project time? What are the pros and cons of each method for your circumstances?

3. What rules of business etiquette for e-mail do you need to adopt that are different from your current techniques?

4. What tools within your e-mail software could you use more effectively to help you organize and prioritize your e-mails and contacts?

5. How might you use social media effectively to increase your digital presence as a lawyer?

6. What aspects of social media do you need to use more carefully to avoid possible violations of your state bar association's professional rules for lawyers?

Time and Work Management Away from the Office

You will spend part of your time out of the office: in court, at the client's site, or during travel. More lawyers are working remotely now because technological advancements make it easy. While out of the office, you need to be productive and capture your billable units.

Determine whether business travel can be effectively avoided by using videoconferencing options for real-time meetings. However, in-person meetings are preferable for interactions that will:

- require lengthy discussions or tense conversations about controversial matters
- require give-and-take negotiations about a matter
- involve interactions with someone with whom you already have a difficult relationship
- involve important one-on-one time to build trust in a new client relationship
- create potential misunderstandings if in-person discussion does not occur

In these instances, you will ultimately spend more time trying to smooth over bad communications if they occur than you would have by traveling to the meeting initially.

Brief your staff members carefully before you leave. Even with top-notch technology, it is not the same as being there. You still want reliable staff to oversee matters and prevent things from falling through the cracks while you are out of the office.

If at all possible, have just one staff member as your point person. That person should be briefed on all current files, be available to field messages to and from others when e-mail or voicemail would not be appropriate or adequate, work with clients directly, and implement your instructions during your absence. If circumstances warrant it, also have a lawyer colleague work with the staff member to oversee your files.

Consider the following matters to make this relationship work smoothly during your absence:

- Leave a detailed itinerary: flights, arrivals and departures, hotels, friends you are staying with, client site locations and appointment times, and emergency numbers.
- Make sure that the staff member has access to your calendar, task lists, and other daily work management tools. With full information, the staff member can coordinate appointments for after your return, handle minor tasks, and know your priorities for work flow. You will be freed up from some of the administrative basics while you are gone if you provide enough information.
- Decide whether you will forward all telephone calls to your smartphone or to a staff member. If you will be out of touch because of travel or client meetings for long stretches, staff may be able to handle matters more promptly than if clients must wait for you to access your messages.
- Decide whether your e-mails will be monitored by a staff member or you will monitor them while you are gone. Your clients may receive more prompt responses if a staff member handles your e-mails and sends only urgent messages to you.
- Make sure that when you are accessing e-mails or taking telephone calls in public places, you are careful about confidentiality and the security of your wireless connection.
- Carefully consider what voicemail message and out-of-office e-mail message you wish to implement to alert clients and others of your availability to return calls and reply to e-mails while traveling. If a staff member will be available, be sure to include that person's details as the contact.
- Alert your staff member as to any people or matters that you consider high priority so that the importance of a telephone call or e-mail from those people is perceived accurately.
- Leave specific written instructions for all matters that you want handled during your absence. How detailed the instructions need to be will depend on whether the staff member routinely works on

that client matter and whether the person is experienced or new as a team member.

- Your written instructions for files that are unfamiliar to the staff member should include the following minimal information:
  - a brief summary of the case and the current status of the file
  - any notes about the specific client: "prefers to be contacted at cell phone number," "is aware the motion may be denied," "can come by to sign documents only on Tuesdays or Thursdays"
  - actions to be completed on the file: "have the client review the draft affidavit with you for possible corrections," "fax the signed document to opposing counsel," "have the law clerk research the first issue indicated in the January 10 client interview notes at point 8"
  - updates you desire while you are gone: "let me know when the client has signed the affidavit," "tell me when the client has received my message"
- Anticipate which other active files may be needed in your absence even though you do not anticipate specific tasks for completion.
  - Give the staff member a list of these files with short status notes, or attach a note to each file about its status.
  - Make sure the staff member knows where the files are located in your office.
- Leave your desk as neat as possible so staff can quickly find files, correspondence, or other items.
- Have set times each day when you will confer with the staff member by telephone. It is important to talk together directly and not depend solely on e-mail, text, or voicemail.
  - It is often faster and more accurate to discuss a matter together than to leave long messages and risk misunderstanding.
  - Some confidential matters may not be appropriate for e-mail, voicemail, or text.
  - Schedule actual times for one call-in for morning, one for midday, and one for the end of the day to avoid telephone tag.

Set times each day when you will return client phone calls and reply to their e-mails. If you can schedule the same times each day, your staff member can indicate when the client can expect a response. You can duplicate the same information on your voicemail and out-of-office e-mail message to indicate your availability to reply. Designate three times during the day; by choosing mid-morning, mid-afternoon, and before the close of business, you will be able to return most calls within roughly two or three hours of when a message was left with a staff member or on your voicemail.

Obviously there will be some matters that will require your more urgent attention. You can reply to those more quickly by checking e-mail and voicemail every half hour or hour. However, by moving routine matters to the designated time, it will allow you to focus on the important tasks at hand rather than fragment your attention.

Even with set times for returning calls and replying to e-mails, make decisions quickly about which ones can be handled later in the day and which ones will get your first attention. Use the same categories discussed in Chapter 4 to prioritize these tasks (most important, important, and least important).

Use care when working on the plane and in the airport. Be cautious about confidentiality and security in these locations. We have all overheard cell phone conversations that should have remained private or seen confidential documents in plain view.

- What level of security is available with the wireless connections and cloud computing you are using?
- Does your laptop have a privacy screen so that the person next to you cannot read your document?
- Are you reading e-mails or texting confidential material on your smartphone that the person next to you might read?
- Are you returning telephone calls that may divulge confidential information within earshot of others?
- Are you discussing a case with another lawyer that someone else may overhear?

- Are you reading confidential papers that the person next to you might casually peruse?

Work on items that are not potentially sensitive if you cannot guarantee confidentiality. Material you need to read for updating is ideal: legal newspapers, articles in your practice area, online CLE segments.

Take precautions when working at the hotel, in a coffee shop, or in other public areas. Be conscious of security issues when using WI-FI in public locations. Even hotel WI-FI is not always fully secure. Using your firm's virtual private network (VPN) is the safest way to stay connected. Be cautious when discussing client matters in a restaurant or coffee shop. Avoid leaving confidential files lying around in your hotel room when you are expecting room service or maid service. Make sure that you stay organized so that papers, flash drives, or other materials are not inadvertently left behind.

Be discreet when working at a client's site. You will likely need to return telephone calls and reference documents on other clients' matters during the day while you are visiting a different client on-site. Be certain that you are in a private area when you do so.

- Ask if there is an empty conference room or unused office that you could borrow for these tasks.
- When leaving the area you have used, double-check that you have left nothing behind that would divulge information about a client.
- Do not spend so much time on other clients' matters that the client you are visiting becomes annoyed by your lack of focus or is offended by your rudeness.

Deal with billing issues effectively. When traveling, it is easy to lose track of billable units if your firm has hourly billing.

- With VPN capabilities, you can use your laptop to record time directly on your office system.
- With a smartphone, you can download one of the time-capture apps to assist you. Some apps can communicate with your office

software; for other apps, you will capture the billable units and convert them to your firm's system on your return.

- Go the old-fashioned route with pad and pen if all else fails.
- Be cognizant of issues regarding billing for travel (varies by client and employer) and double-billing.

Consider these general tips regarding travel. You want to make the time away from the office productive and hassle free.

- Apply for frequent flyer and rewards cards for airlines, hotels, and rental car companies. Use these numbers whenever appropriate within your firm's travel policies.
- If available, only use an employer's credit card for travel arrangements and expenses. Alternatively, use the employer's travel consultant (internal staff member or external travel agent) for all travel arrangements so that payment is through the employer rather than on your personal credit card.
- If you must use your personal credit card and apply for reimbursements, use one credit card just for business travel so you know everything on the monthly statement gets reimbursed. Another advantage is that your personal spending preferences will not be revealed to your employer if you lose a receipt and have to provide a credit card statement instead.
- Ask your employer's travel consultant to keep your travel preferences on file: aisle seat, eight rows maximum from an exit, extra leg room, special meal requirements, airlines and airports to avoid, shuttle versus taxicab, times of day for departing and returning flights, nonsmoking room, king-size bed. Also have your various frequent flyer and club reward numbers on file.
- File any travel reimbursement forms as soon as possible on your return. If you are prompt, you are less likely to lose receipts or forget to include items that are reimbursable. Some organizations will refuse reimbursement if receipts are not turned in within a certain number of days after travel.

- For frequent travelers, preplanning can make trips less stressful:
  - Have a prestocked briefcase used only for business travel with everything you will need: legal pads, pens, stapler, batteries, file folders, extra flash drive, etc.
  - Have a prestocked suitcase used only for business travel with the basics you will need: umbrella, toiletries, shoe shine kit, first aid items, cold medicine, prescriptions, etc.
  - Have a standard checklist for travel that includes the items you want to have with you for any trip.
  - Take a large envelope with you to collect in one place all receipts and notes regarding reimbursement.
  - If you are reimbursed for mileage and parking, keep a list of common distances and rates that you need:
    - miles between home and the airport parking garage
    - miles between the firm and the offices of frequently visited clients
    - daily rate at the airport parking garage
  - Have a list of people who can handle all the personal items while you are on the road: dog sitter or kennels, neighbor to water your plants, childcare options, house sitter.
  - Have preprinted instructions to give these same people explaining pet care, plant care, mail pick-up, package delivery, or other matters.
  - Have a list of emergency contact information for these same people: veterinary clinic, medical offices, alarm-monitoring company, neighbors, nearest relative.

By being more organized when you work away from the office, you can minimize the hassles of working remotely. You can combine the smart use of technology with strong staff support to manage your time well and maintain high productivity.

Reflection and Strategies

1. When you will be out of the office and need to make sure that staff members and other attorneys know your whereabouts, consider the following aspects:
    a. Which people need to have the information and which do not need it?
    b. What information is relevant for them to know without divulging more than necessary?
    c. Where does your employer draw the line as to time that is your personal time and time that the firm can interrupt?
2. In what ways do you need to be more careful during travel about client confidentiality than you have been in the past?
3. If you are not efficient in capturing your billing units while out of the office, what steps do you need to take for greater effectiveness: apps for your smartphone, VPN interface, pad and pen?
4. What preplanning and organizing steps can you undertake to make your business trips less stressful?

Additional Commitments You Must Manage

Your list of other commitments will include firm committees, firm social events, pro bono work, and community responsibilities. All these extra obligations have to be managed carefully to balance them effectively with your other daily professional duties. With wise time and work management, these additional commitments can enhance your career rather than create additional burdens.

OBLIGATIONS AS A COMMITTEE MEMBER OR CHAIRPERSON

Many law firms have a mix of junior and senior lawyers on their committees. As a committee member, do not underestimate the importance of your role. A strong performance on a committee can enhance your reputation as a team player and provide you with experience for later chairperson responsibilities.

Consider these tips for committee members. You want your performance as a member to signal your full commitment to the tasks assigned to the committee. Implement the following points to become known as a positive committee member:

- Always show up on time for meetings. Lateness reflects poorly on your ability to manage your obligations, and it signals disrespect for your colleagues.
- Always arrive fully prepared for the meetings. Bring with you all documents that will be discussed. Be ready to take notes regarding any assignments you are given or information you will need to reference later.
- Keep your comments during the meeting succinct and on topic. Do not wander to other matters that are peripheral and not on the agenda.
- If a meeting gets bogged down, move it forward with a summary of the discussion so far, a question to get to the next point of discussion, or a rules-of-order question.

- Do not work on unrelated tasks during the meeting: reviewing client letters, reading articles, texting clients, reading e-mail on your tablet. Multitasking is rude and indicates to others that you think the meeting is a waste of time.
- Complete any assigned tasks beforehand and organize any presentation that you must give so that it will be succinct and professional.
  - Speak from notes or an outline if you are likely to get flustered.
  - Have handouts, a PowerPoint, charts, or spreadsheets as appropriate to help members follow your presentation.
  - Distribute complex or lengthy materials before the meeting to facilitate prior review by committee members.
  - Arrange several days ahead for any audiovisual capabilities or other support needed for your presentation.
- Schedule sufficient time on your calendar to attend the entire meeting and do not gather up your belongings before the chairperson adjourns the meeting. Preparing to leave before the meeting is adjourned is rude and signals to others that you do not care what else is discussed.

After you have more experience at the firm, you will want to secure opportunities to show leadership as a committee chairperson. The organizational and leadership skills you exhibit as the chairperson will determine whether the committee's work progresses smoothly. Success in chairing even a minor committee prepares you for more important assignments in the future.

Consider these tips for committee chairpersons. You want your committee to be praised for accomplishing its tasks in an organized and timely manner. The following points will assist you in your success as a chairperson:

- Give careful thought to the charge to the committee, the specific tasks to be accomplished, the deadlines to be met, the authority of the committee, budgetary matters, and the membership of the committee.

- Consider the status of the committee: a standing committee, a subcommittee, or an ad hoc committee.
  - Standing committees are integral to the firm's committee structure and will have greater purview, more power, and longer-term commitments.
  - Subcommittees are organized under the umbrella of another committee for specific subtasks, will only have advisory power to the parent committee, and often have limited duration.
  - Ad hoc committees are organized for specific tasks, will often have advisory power rather than decision-making power, and have limited duration.
- If the charge to the committee is unclear, get more information by discussing it with the managing partner.
- Understand the exact outcomes that the committee is expected to accomplish through its work.
- Determine whether the committee is accomplishing tasks within a predetermined budget (example: the Marketing Committee has $50,000 to expend on new marketing initiatives) or if the committee is charged with proposing a budget for future expenditures (example: the Marketing Committee will propose $50,000 of new marketing initiatives to the Management Committee).
- If committee members have already been assigned, determine any specific expertise or expressed interest related to those assignment decisions.
- If you will select committee members, determine your methods: personal invitation, general solicitation of interest, ex officio membership, supervisor input on lawyer membership.
- If at all possible, schedule regular committee meetings so that members have all future dates and times on their calendars (example: third Friday of the month at 3:00 p.m. for one hour).
- Calendar the meetings electronically for whatever future time period seems reasonable (the next three months, six months, or

the entire year). A meeting can always be canceled if it does not need to be held as previously calendared.

- Complete the meeting within the time scheduled. A set time frame encourages members to arrive promptly, prevents discussions from rambling, and alerts everyone to the specific amount of time in which to complete the agenda. If possible, limit a meeting to one hour.
- Solicit agenda items for the meeting ahead of time if appropriate.
- Send a finalized agenda out to the members several days ahead of the meeting. Indicate on the agenda any individuals responsible for specific agenda items. Provide any documents that members should review in preparation for attendance.
- Ask a committee member or staff member (if the meeting is not confidential) to take minutes. Distribute the draft minutes for review as soon as possible after the meeting. Send out the finalized minutes before the next scheduled meeting.
- Begin the meeting exactly on time to alert members to the expectation that they not wander in late. If a member consistently arrives late, discuss the matter privately with that person and request prompt attendance.
- Work through the agenda in the order specified in that document unless there is a good reason to discuss items out of order. Put the most important items on the agenda at the beginning. Guest speakers should also be earlier in the agenda if possible.
- Move on to the next agenda item only after the current item has been discussed fully, acted upon, or tabled for future discussion.
- Keep discussions on track. If members get off topic, steer the discussion back to the agenda item. Suggest that peripheral discussions be completed outside the meeting or scheduled as agenda items for future meetings.
- After an agenda item is completed, summarize the decision or actions to be taken. If actions are needed, delineate who will complete which tasks and by what dates. Ask for questions before moving on to the next item.

- Have a basic familiarity with *Robert's Rules of Order* to keep the procedures of the committee organized.
- If you need audiovisual or videoconferencing capabilities or other support for the meeting, arrange for it several days in advance.

SOCIAL EVENTS: THE FIRM AND THE LOCAL LEGAL COMMUNITY

Some lawyers thrive on social interactions with senior lawyers and partners at firm events. Other lawyers would rather be elsewhere interacting with family and friends or quietly relaxing at home.

Realize that attendance at social events shows your support for the firm and impacts your future there. Meeting your billable-hour target and doing competent work are necessary, but being known by the partners in the firm is also important. Network with as many senior lawyers and partners as possible rather than talking with only other associates.

Why is networking with senior members of the firm so important? Imagine that your firm decides to lay off some associates. If the decision is between two lawyers with equal billable hours and expertise, the one that all the partners know and like will stay, and the one that some of the partners do not know will leave. If the decision instead were about a plum assignment, the same truth would likely hold. Your future with the firm can be determined not only by objective criteria but also by subjective criteria.

You may be asked to fill an empty seat at the firm's sponsored table for a local bar event. These events will offer you networking opportunities as well as lots of free meals. Once again, you will be seen as supportive of the firm if you make yourself available for these opportunities.

Social events sponsored by local bar groups are also important for general networking opportunities. You will want to meet the lawyers who are in your practice specialty, who are potential mentors, and who are active in the local legal community. Local judges and law professors also attend many bar events.

Read a business etiquette book before you go out on the legal social circuit. Unlike prior generations of lawyers, many younger lawyers have not been taught basic business etiquette. You need to exhibit impeccable manners at all times. What works with your friends will not work with a group of judges or senior lawyers.

PRO BONO CASES WITHIN YOUR WORKLOAD

Each law firm has its own policies and attitudes toward pro bono work. Find out your firm's parameters: minimum or maximum hours, the impact on your billable-hour total, required firm procedures or reporting mechanisms.

When accepting pro bono cases, be realistic as you evaluate your expertise and your available time. Estimate the number of hours you will need to commit to each case. If you will not have staff assistance, factor in the extra time that routine, administrative tasks may take you.

SERVICE THROUGH BAR ASSOCIATIONS AND COMMUNITY ORGANIZATIONS

Many lawyers are active in their local, regional, and state bar groups. Newer lawyers often get involved with a young lawyers association. Specialty bar organizations provide a great way to network with lawyers who are experts in your practice area and potential mentors. Committee work and task forces equip you with leadership skills. Service projects run the gamut from running pro bono clinics to teaching Street Law at the high school to collecting teddy bears for children in adoption proceedings. Writing opportunities for a local bar newsletter or state bar magazine may also exist.

Local nonprofit and corporate groups often ask lawyers to serve in board positions. These positions may or may not require you to provide legal advice to the group. Be aware of any policies your firm has about accepting board positions. When considering a board position, you want to weigh any potential problems with attorney-client privilege, conflicts of interest with firm clients, and financial disclosures. Make sure you understand the parameters of the position, the duties you are expected to fulfill, the time commitments, and the length of time you will serve in the position.

Remember to save room in your schedule for community service through volunteerism and local service organizations. Your service may be volunteer hours for a nonlegal cause dear to your heart: tutoring on your lunch hour at a local elementary school, coaching in the youth soccer league, building a local Habitat for Humanity house, or leading your church choir.

Lawyers are often the backbone of community groups, especially in smaller locales. You will gain a great deal of personal satisfaction from these opportunities. In addition, lawyers who are active in the greater community provide good publicity for the profession.

Lawyers often become members in service organizations such as Rotary, Kiwanis, or Lions Club. These organizations provide networking opportunities with local political leaders, businessmen, and potential clients. Leadership skills can be honed through officer and committee positions. These groups regularly participate in fund-raisers and service projects, which provide you with additional chances to give back to the local community. Opportunities for regional, state, or national involvement also exist with these service organizations.

If you efficiently and effectively handle the extra opportunities available both inside and outside your firm, you can gain professional skills as well as personal satisfaction. If you become an expert at the time and work management strategies discussed in the earlier chapters, you will participate in these additional commitments without feeling overwhelmed or stressed.

Reflection and Strategies

1. If you are the chairperson of a committee, what changes could you make to be more effective in your role and to increase the productivity of the committee?
2. If you are a committee member, what changes in your attitude or behavior would make you a more positive and productive committee member?

3. Are you making the most out of networking opportunities at firm and bar association social events? If not, how can you increase your skill at networking?
4. If you are not currently involved in pro bono cases, consider why not. How might you become more involved if you value that lawyering commitment?
5. What bar association and community organization activities would contribute to your service and networking opportunities?
6. How do you plan to balance those professional aspects with the personal responsibilities that you have?
7. What committee assignments, bar association duties, board positions, community service projects, or other outside commitments should be indicated on your resume?

Additional Comments for Non-firm Lawyers

Whether you are working for a judge, a government agency, a corporation, or a nonprofit, you need to manage your time and work responsibilities efficiently and effectively. The information in the prior chapters will translate equally to your position with a non-firm employer. However, here are specific thoughts for lawyers outside the law firm environment.

THE JUDICIAL CLERK POSITION

- Learn the hierarchy within the judicial administrative staff. The setup will be different depending on your court: federal or state, trial or appellate, rural or urban, one location or satellite locations. Whether the person in charge of administrative and staff duties is a clerk, staff lawyer, or administrator, you need to rely on that person for guidance. In some situations, your direct supervision will come from a judge or several judges; however, in larger court settings, you may have more daily contact with the administrative staff than the judges.
- Learn where you fit into the hierarchy. Are there first-year and second-year judicial clerks with separate duties? Are there multiple judicial clerks working for your judge? Are there multiple judges for whom you will work? Will you also complete work for court personnel?
- Learn the etiquette and procedures for your court. How do you address court personnel as well as judicial personnel? Are there restricted areas within the courthouse? What are the security procedures you must follow?
- Learn the expectations of your judge. What are the preferences that the judge has regarding various tasks that you will perform, such as researching, writing, and drafting? Every judge also has expectations about court etiquette and proper procedures. Learn what behaviors and habits irritate your particular judge and diligently avoid them.

- Take advantage of this unique learning opportunity to strengthen your credentials for future legal positions. Although law clerks are selected from the best students that law schools produce, they are still new lawyers and have a great deal to learn about research, writing, legal analysis, the legal system, and time and work management. Observe more experienced judicial clerks and staff to learn how to organize your work better. Request constructive feedback on your projects when appropriate.
- You will be expected to be a "jack of all trades and master of none" as a judicial clerk, unless you are working for a limited jurisdiction court. The variety of legal assignments will be challenging at times because of your lack of prior academic or practice background in many topic areas. Realize that you will need extra time for background research before you begin some assignments.
- Make a file for each assignment and keep all your notes, copies of cases/statutes read (even if not used), and your research tracking form.[1] You may get a similar or related assignment at a later time, and this background file will save you time on the new project.
- Your work products may be excellent writing samples for future job applications. However, you will need to get permission to use them in this way and will need to redact identifying information as appropriate. Your work products may also be valuable background research for your practice area after your clerkship.
- Realize that your judicial clerk position will unlikely become permanent no matter how exceptional you are in your role. Improve as a lawyer as much as you can during your clerkship. You want to build a solid reputation with the staff and judges in your courthouse so that you will have excellent recommendations.
- It is not uncommon for an exceptional judicial clerk to move on to employment as a judicial clerk at another court "higher" in the judicial hierarchy after his or her first judicial clerkship. For example, a state judicial clerk may apply for a federal clerkship next.

---

1. See Chapter 7 regarding the use of a research tracking form.

- One of the perquisites for some judicial clerks is the opportunity to attend judicial conferences or seminars for CLE credit; take advantage of these learning and networking opportunities if they come your way.

THE GOVERNMENT POSITION

- Learn the hierarchy of your government agency or department. Know the organizational chart within that governmental unit. What are the legal specialties? Who are the lawyers in those specialties? What is the administrative structure? What other nonlegal areas are there? How does your unit fit into the overall agency?
- Learn how your position fits into the overall scheme of things. What is the reporting hierarchy in your office? Who are your colleagues? How do their duties relate to yours? Who are the staff members for your area? Which other units will you interact with on a regular basis?
- Learn the political impacts of government on your daily work life. Many lawyers work at their tasks without much impact from the comings and goings of political appointees at the top. However, there are always political undercurrents. Know how those undercurrents may impact your work through budget, rivalries, policies, and trends.
- You may have a very specialized area with limited responsibility initially. However, unlike your law school classmates in the Big Law trenches, you will get independent work, greater responsibility, and interesting opportunities much more quickly. If your unit is understaffed and overworked, you will hit the ground running hard and need to master time and work management quickly.
- If you are assigned to a specialized area in which you have limited prior exposure, make sure that you learn your area immediately. Ask your supervisor and other more experienced lawyers for guidance. Request attendance at appropriate continuing legal education seminars to accelerate your learning curve.
- Even though you do not have to bill hours for a client, be aware that you still need to be efficient with your time and work organ-

ization. Until you become familiar with how long various tasks take, keep a log. You will be able to estimate time more accurately for similar projects in the future if you noted how long the earlier project took you.

- Watch for cutting-edge areas that are developing in the law. You may be able to volunteer for a new specialty area once you have proven yourself as competent and reliable. New legal areas allow you to gain expertise and job opportunities that might not otherwise open up as early in your career.

THE IN-HOUSE COUNSEL

- Whether you work for a corporation, nonprofit organization, university, or other institution, it is your responsibility to protect that entity's best interests. You will be better able to advise the entity on legal matters if you fully understand its business strategies. The better matched you are with that entity's goals and values, the more comfortable you will be in your work. Spend time learning about your client's mission, strategic plan, prospectus, business operations, marketing materials, etc.
- If you are a member of a multi-lawyer legal department, you need to understand how you fit into the scheme: hierarchical distinctions, reporting lines, and the practice areas you will cover. Size of the legal department will greatly influence your assigned work and, therefore, your time and work management strategies.
- If you are a one-person legal office, you will decide which legal matters you will handle entirely in-house and which matters you will refer to outside counsel. Be careful about overextending yourself by retaining legal work for which you do not have the expertise or for which you do not have the time.
- Use your budget for hiring outside counsel wisely. Require outside counsel to present a detailed budget for each project. Evaluate "value for money" on every project completed by outside counsel. Be ready to negotiate better terms and to hire different outside counsel if necessary.

- Even though you do not have to bill hours for a client, be aware that you still need to be efficient with your time and work organization. Until you become familiar with how long various tasks take, keep a log. You will be able to estimate time more accurately for similar projects in the future if you noted how long the earlier project took you.
- If your employer hires knowledge management and librarian staff, get to know those staff members well. They can often help you find information more quickly.

The work environments of non-firm lawyers often have tremendous benefits that impact quality of life, time management, and work organization. A few of those benefits include:

- more control over one's work schedule and ability to predict hours with typically fewer overtime hours required on a regular basis
- no billing targets to meet, though other measures may apply (number of completed matters, timeliness of completion, or budgetary savings)
- more extensive electronic database, librarian, or knowledge management resources
- for many government and in-house lawyers, more complex matters and a broader range of issues at earlier points in their careers
- for judicial clerks, extensive research and writing experience with insights into judicial decision making while learning lawyering skills in a supportive environment

The variety of legal environments outside the private practice of law offers many challenges and rewards. For many lawyers, the quality-of-life characteristics of non-firm practice are a positive trade-off for the high salaries earned by law firm colleagues and the stress of the quest for partnership.

Reflection and Strategies

1. If you are currently a judicial clerk, list the new skills you have acquired already in that position and the additional skills you want to acquire before moving to the next legal employer.

2. How does your non-firm employment fit into your long-term goals as a lawyer? Is it a stepping stone to another career path in the law or have you found your niche?

3. If you have moved to a non-firm employer after private practice, what are the differences that strengthen your job satisfaction as a lawyer, and what are the challenges of your new position?

Additional Comments for Solo Practitioners

Solo practitioners have especially important decisions to make about time and work management to ensure their success in legal practice. You will want to access the many resources provided by the American Bar Association, state bars, and legal blogs to learn how to manage your solo practice more efficiently and effectively and to expand your time and work management options through technology. Here are some solo practice tips to supplement the prior chapters in this book.

SETTING UP YOUR OFFICE AND WORKSPACE

- You may be tempted to start out initially from a home office to save costs. However, most of us do not have an ideal living situation to accommodate a law office.
  - A separate entrance and office space within your home will give your practice a greater air of professionalism than expecting your client to walk through your living room or kitchen to get to the office.
  - Some clients, especially those of the opposite sex, may be nervous about meeting with a lawyer in a home environment.
  - Confidentiality of your client conversations, voicemails, documents, and computer files may be at risk unless your office area is completely off limits to family members.
  - Lease provisions, homeowner's association bylaws, or local zoning ordinances may prevent your setting up an office in your home.
- Virtual law offices are gaining some popularity among technologically adept lawyers. In many cases, however, these lawyers still rent conference room space for client meetings.
- You may find another lawyer who will trade available office space in return for your working on that firm's cases as needed. How-

ever, these arrangements can be unsatisfactory if not carefully negotiated.

- You would not want to enter this type of arrangement without very specific written terms.
  - Define your exact time commitments in return for the office space. The other lawyer's demands on your time could conflict with your own client deadlines and projects.
  - Define any access to other spaces in the office suite (reception area, conference room, kitchen, storage), equipment use (phone and data lines, photocopier, scanner, fax), library use (hard copy as well as electronic databases), staff assistance (occasional or not at all), and other considerations that match the environment.
- Make sure that clients know that the two law firms are separate entities so that ethical concerns do not develop.
- Another version of office sharing has become very popular. Several solo lawyers rent a space that provides shared common areas (conference room, reception area, workroom, kitchen, bathrooms, storage space) as well as separate offices for each solo law firm (a lawyer office, a secretary or paralegal office, and possibly a smaller conference space). The flexibility and amenities will depend on square footage and monthly rent.
  - The separate solo firms share the rent for the overall space as well as utilities (if not included in the rent).
  - The separate solo firms may share the costs for a multifunction photocopier/scanner/fax lease, basic non-logo office supplies, security system monitoring, and cleaning services.
  - Each solo firm will set up its own accounts for items that are complicated to share (subscriptions for electronic research databases, credit card machine leases).
  - Each solo firm will often hire its own staff so there will not be conflicts for paralegal or secretarial assistance when both firms have urgent deadlines.
  - The solo firms will make sure that clients know the law firms are separate entities so that ethical concerns do not develop.

- When renting office space, always consider access for disabled clients: parking, elevator, doorframe width, and restrooms.
- You will need to make your office space presentable for clients:
  - Fresh paint, steam-cleaned carpets, and off-the-rack window treatments can inexpensively transform an office space into a professional environment.
  - Gently used office furniture is a more affordable option. Look for sources such as local lawyers who are retiring, businesses that are closing, government surplus items being auctioned to the public, or thrift shops selling higher-quality items. Also visit furniture consignment stores in your area.
  - Renting office furniture temporarily can be a good option, but rent-to-buy contracts are usually expensive.
  - Public areas need to be professional, attractive, and neat—including the restrooms.
  - First impressions matter: carefully chosen artwork, plants, and decorative items can transform your office's message from "new lawyer without an income" to "new lawyer with a successful practice."
  - For many clients, law books on the shelves indicate a successful lawyer because the clients are unaware that electronic research is the norm. You can purchase law reporter sets to grace your shelves from retiring lawyers or law firms and libraries that have switched to electronic sources.
- Determine what amenities you wish to offer your clients: coffee or tea, soda or bottled water, and snacks. You will need a kitchen with a refrigerator, a coffeemaker, and other items to match your preferences.
- If your clients are likely to bring their children with them, be prepared to keep the children occupied while you have an uninterrupted (hopefully) meeting with their parents.
  - If you have a staff member available to monitor their safety, the children can wait in a separate space equipped with toys and a television.

- Otherwise, have a space within your own office where children can draw or play with their toys. Keep a few inexpensive coloring books, sketch pads, crayon packs, or other items available in case the parents do not bring items with them to keep their children occupied.

STAFFING FOR YOUR PRACTICE

- You may initially be the paralegal, secretary, file clerk, and billing clerk as well as the lawyer for your firm. However, you will exhaust yourself and get little lawyering done if you work this way for very long. Even with technology, you cannot do it all.
- Until you can hire permanent staff, use techniques that allow uninterrupted time to work on projects or meet with clients.
  - Have voicemail or an answering machine record your messages. With the latter, protect confidentiality by making sure messages cannot be overheard in the reception area or while you meet with a client in your office.
  - Alternatively, have an answering service take your calls. This option costs more money but provides a live presence for clients. Careful instructions on handling your client calls can alleviate any concerns you have about an answering service that has mostly nonlawyer accounts.
  - Find a law student, relative, or friend to answer the telephones and act as receptionist for several hours each day while you are at court, in client appointments, or working on projects.
  - Schedule client appointments for only three or four days a week so that the remaining time can be used for court appearances or legal projects.
  - Keep a minimum of one day a week entirely clear if possible for concentrated project time.
  - If you are in an office-share situation, you may occasionally ask the other solo's paid staff member to take messages as a favor. However, do not overuse this option if you are not contributing to that staff member's salary.

- Once you can afford to hire staff, consider your specific needs carefully before you advertise and hire.
  - Can you afford to hire a full-time person or a part-time person?
  - Can you afford to hire someone with a salary and benefits or just an hourly-wage employee with limited benefits?
  - Do you need someone who will occasionally work overtime, or will you be able to survive with a strictly nine-to-five person?
  - Do you need a secretary or a paralegal? Unless your business is substantial, you may actually benefit more from the former rather than the latter as an initial hire.
  - Write a job description before you advertise or begin interviewing.
    - You need to be clear about your expectations, and the applicants will need to have specific information.
    - Be sure to include a catch-all phrase in the job description, such as "other duties as assigned," for the inevitable tasks you will forget or which will develop as your practice grows and changes.
  - Consider the time it will take you to train someone in the position.
    - You will need to provide more training for someone unfamiliar with law firms than for someone with law firm credentials.
    - Even an experienced staff person will need training on your specific expectations and office systems.
    - You will need a training plan and materials: office manual, one-on-one sessions, templates for documents, technology training, and more.
- Consider what other staff or services you will need:
  - Bookkeeper, accountant, or CPA
  - Agency to handle payroll or your hiring through an employment agency that takes care of payroll
- Consider what additional staff assistance you might be able to hire inexpensively or get for free.

* Does a local law school have upper-division students who can be hired for research and drafting projects?
* Does a local college have an internship program for pre-law majors? These students may be able to do court runs, filing, photocopying, and other routine office tasks.
* Does a local high school have a law magnet program for pre-law students? These students may also be able to assist with routine office tasks.
* Does a local graduate program have upper-division accounting students who can assist you with basic bookkeeping and billing tasks?

Remember that no matter what types of staff you ultimately hire, there are two important considerations:

* Include extensive training on professionalism and confidentiality for all staff members—law students, volunteers, interns, and hired staff.
* You are ultimately responsible for work products that come out of your office. You need to review every letter, document, and other piece of paper carefully. You are the quality assurance officer for your firm even when your staff members are very competent.

THE PURELY ADMINISTRATIVE DECISIONS
* Do not underestimate how time consuming it will be to push the paper through your firm and to manage routine tasks.
* You need to organize at least the following work management aspects of your office:
  * What document assembly software (if one is available for your jurisdiction and specialty) will you use to make drafting easier?
  * What additional templates will you have to create for letters, standard instructions, client contracts, client payment plans, and other practice documents?
  * What system will you use to calendar your appointments, court dates, discovery deadlines, statutes of limitation, and more?

- ○ How will you back up these systems so that you have both hard-copy and electronic versions?
- ○ What software will you use to synchronize your calendar with your smartphone?
- What method will you use to track your time, and will that system be able to interface with your billing software?
- What manual or electronic system will you set up for your client files?
- What systems will you use to track conflicts of interest for inquiries and for clients?
- What system will you use to keep client contact information readily available?
- What system will you use to easily track and monitor client payments?
- Will you use the U.S. Postal Service for your postage requirements or other Internet websites?
- Will you use local printers or Internet sources for your printing needs with your firm logo (letterhead, envelopes, business cards, postcards, firm holiday greeting cards, labels, notepads, and more)?
- What combination of local businesses and Internet sources will you use for your marketing (logo design, website design, signage for the firm, newspaper ads, TV and radio ads, phonebook ads, legal directories, other marketing tools)?
- What firm website and social media presence do you want to have?
- Determine your billing methods and fees carefully:
  - Find out what other solo lawyers are charging for the types of work that you undertake.
    - ○ Do they charge hourly rates or fixed fees for the work?
    - ○ How do the charges vary based on differences among those firms: practice experience of the solo and level of staff assistance?
    - ○ What other variables would make those charges appropriate or inappropriate for your own legal work?

- Monitor how many hours it takes you to do a particular type of work. If your typical range of hours can be carefully determined, you will be able to set fixed fees more accurately.
- Several times a year, review your fees and adjust them as needed to reflect any changes in your practice.
  - Have your time expenditures for particular types of work decreased as you have gained experience?
  - Has your level of expertise increased so that you may charge more than you previously could?
  - Has your level of expertise allowed you to expand into more complex matters for which you should increase your fees?
  - Do increased staffing costs with the growth of your practice need to be reflected in your fees?
  - Have fees for other lawyers in your area increased or decreased?
- Evaluate your work regularly for ways in which you can become more efficient and effective in your time and work management. These changes can improve the bottom line of your firm.

LEGAL RESEARCH

- Look for free legal research tools for public data, business intelligence, court cases, statutes, and more.
- If you purchase a subscription for an electronic research database, negotiate a customized package that includes only the jurisdictions and specialty areas that are important to your practice. Make sure you understand the cost differentials for different databases and any add-on costs for technical support, training, printing, or occasional use of other databases outside your subscription package.
- Consider whether there are other libraries in the area that you can use for research: courthouses, law schools, or legal collections in public libraries.
- Consider hiring law students to complete at least some of your legal research at a much lower fee to your client than your own charges would be.

PRO BONO CASES

- Determine how many pro bono cases you can realistically handle and still meet all your personal and professional financial obligations. You must pay your bills and take care of your family's needs.
- Determine how many pro bono cases you can realistically handle and still meet your obligations to your paying clients as well as manage your law practice.
- Decide what criteria you will use to determine whether you will accept a case pro bono. Remember that accepting a case pro bono up front is different from *allowing* a case to end up as pro bono work.
- Practice your compassionate but firm statement for declining to take a case pro bono. In addition, practice responses to any client objections that you anticipate when you decline a case.
- Keep a reference list of phone numbers and addresses as suggestions for clients you turn away: legal aid, other low-cost or nonprofit legal assistance, and lawyers who do pro bono cases in practice areas that you do not cover.

NETWORKING, COMMUNITY SERVICE, AND OTHER COMMITMENTS

- As a solo practitioner, you need to balance time in the office and court, time for building your practice, and time for yourself.
- Determine your availability to become involved in local networking and service opportunities.
  - During the first years of practice, you may need to settle for mere membership and attendance at events.
  - As you have more time and your practice is better established, consider volunteering for committees and running for elected positions.
- Join the local bar association and specialty practice groups.
  - You will develop contacts with other solo practitioners who may refer clients outside their own practice areas.
  - You will develop relationships with experienced lawyers who can answer questions and offer advice.

- You will meet local government lawyers, law professors, and judges.
- Attend local CLE programs to expand your legal knowledge and to meet expert lawyers who can offer advice in your practice area.
- Attend statewide CLE programs to expand your legal knowledge and to meet other lawyers and experts in your practice area outside your geographical region.
- Attend CLE programs to expand your knowledge and expertise in law practice management and legal technology.
- Join the local chapter for your state's young lawyers association if you are new to the profession. In addition to having another support system, you will meet your own generation of practitioners who will be colleagues throughout your career.
- You can make valuable client contacts through various local community groups: a service organization, church, charity, sports league, or political party.

The life of a solo practitioner can be challenging, exciting, and overwhelming at the same time. You will be less overwhelmed as you become more accomplished at time and work management strategies.

Reflection and Strategies

1. What are the pros and cons of your current office location and organizational model? Do you need to make changes to increase your visibility or expand your practice areas?
2. Is your current staffing model the best one for your practice? What changes do you need to make in personnel, training, or outside service contracts to optimize your own time and meet the demands of your practice?

3. What software or other systems do you need to adopt to streamline the many administrative aspects of your solo practice?
4. What additional marketing strategies do you need to adopt to increase referrals from other lawyers and expand your client base?
5. Does your current fee structure accurately reflect your level of expertise, complexities of your workload, and overhead costs? How do your fees compare with other lawyers in your local area?
6. Do you have the proper balance among building your practice, completing work for clients, and having personal time? If not, where do you need to make adjustments? What strategies can help you reach the optimal balance?

Balancing Your Professional and Personal Lives

When you start to practice law, it is easy to succumb to arriving early and staying late at the office every day. Drafting documents takes longer because you have never done them before. When researching you must gain background knowledge in the legal topic before you can start any billable research. Your projects frequently involve other lawyers' files, for which you have to gain context before you can begin your work product.

The pressure on new lawyers is enormous: billing targets to retain their jobs and get bonuses, constant scrutiny of their work by more-senior lawyers with limited or nonexistent feedback, internal doubts about one's competence while trying to appear confident, attempts to fit into a firm culture that is not always transparent. Add to those pressures the realities of law firm layoffs, client readiness to switch firms, and the firm's possible outsourcing of work. New lawyers realize quickly that if their work products are not excellent, more-complex and more-lucrative work will not be allotted to them.

If a lawyer is single and without a social network in a new city, the temptation to be a workaholic becomes greater. No one is waiting at home or expecting the lawyer for a social engagement. Staying late and plowing through another file or document draft seems logical.

These early habits of a new lawyer easily carry over as the lawyer becomes more experienced. The pressures now include committee work, desire for partnership, increased lifestyle expectations, and more. Client load will increase as well as the complexity of the client matters handled. More work than can be dealt with in a normal workday or week continues.

Lawyers who are married struggle to complete the workload and arrive home at some semi-reasonable time. Once children are added to the mix, the challenges for a home life become greater. And if the lawyer is a single parent, the struggle includes finding safe and appropriate childcare as well as being an engaged parent in the family hours remaining once the workday is over.

Make a list of personal values to refocus on what is really important to you. Your value list should include your *internal* values. Examples might be fairness, personal growth, a healthy lifestyle, service to others, compassion, love, empathy, integrity, spiritual growth, and close friendships. Exclude from your list values that are *external* and dependent on comparing yourself to others: wealth, fame, prestige, success. External values ultimately provide less lasting satisfaction than internal values. In addition, the trappings that support those external values can be easily destroyed by a stock-market crash, job loss, or other unexpected event. Carefully consider the internal values that you hold dear and use the worksheet to list them.

• •

Personal Values Worksheet

The following values are integral to my life and provide me with lasting satisfaction:

1.

2.

3.

4.

5.

6.

7.

8.

9.

10.

[Add as many values as are relevant to your life.]

Hopefully, many of these values will be reflected in both your work and home environments. Ideally, you want your work-life balance to allow time to include these important values on a regular basis. Read your value list at least once a month to remind yourself of these values. Re-center your life as soon as you realize you are no longer in balance. If you routinely find that you do not have opportunities to integrate your values in your work and your personal life, you may need to give serious thought to changes in your lifestyle.

Set personal goals in addition to any professional goals. If you do not set goals for your personal life, your professional goals are likely to consume all your time and energy. Your personal goals may include interaction with family and friends; however, you also need personal goals focusing just on *you* as an individual.

By achieving your personal goals, you will attain a work-life balance that will provide you with more satisfaction, improve your personal relationships, and increase your energy for your professional life. Consider the following areas for possible personal goals:

- volunteering each week or month for a community group that is close to your heart
- taking up a new hobby that you have always wanted to start
- exercising each week with personal objectives for strength training, weight loss, or other benefits
- renewing your spiritual roots by attending a church, synagogue, or temple
- joining a reading group and discussing one nonlegal book a month that you have read
- teaching your child a skill or sport that you can enjoy together
- reserving one weekday evening each week for family or friends
- reserving regular weekend time each week for family or friends
- reserving one Friday or Monday each month when you will take a long three-day weekend
- planning your vacation ahead and actually taking the time rather than forgetting to take it or canceling it because of work

Look at the personal values in your worksheet and write two goals for implementing each of those values into your personal life on a regular basis. The goals should be realistic, specific, and measurable. From the list, select the one goal you wish to achieve first. Limit your focus to just one goal so that you will not get discouraged and give up.

Write down the strategies and tasks that you will use to reach the goal. Include the measures that will determine whether you have attained your goal. These steps are similar to the exercise you completed in Chapter 4 for your professional goal setting. A sample worksheet is provided.

Evaluate your progress on your goal each month and continue to work on it until it is met. Congratulate yourself on any goal that has become a regular part of your work-life balance and then select a new goal from your list.

Use your allotted benefits to gain greater work-life balance. Every organization has rules about personal time: vacation accrual, compensatory time, personal days, and coverage during a lawyer's absence. You obviously need to follow your employer's procedures. Give the proper notice, arrange the appropriate coverage, and hand in the correct paperwork.

Take the leave time that you accrue. You ultimately harm yourself if you do not take necessary sick days, vacation time, and personal days. Working at the office when you are contagious with the flu lengthens your own illness and infects others. Skipping vacation until you lose days that can no longer be carried over helps the firm's bottom line but not your stress level or blood pressure. Not taking a personal day when your spouse faces a crisis ignores your family responsibilities.

Decide the appropriate times for you to arrive at and leave the office given your firm's culture. Watch to see what the other lawyers do and determine the common patterns. If lawyers drift in during the 8:00–8:45 a.m. time frame for a 9:00 a.m. opening, then you can do the same. If the lawyers all leave by 5:30 p.m. on a regular basis, then you can as well. If none of the lawyers leave until everyone senior has left, then that is your firm's culture.

• •

Strategies, Tasks, and Measures for a Personal Goal

GOAL: Provide service to others.

STRATEGY 1: Determine what hours per week could be devoted to service to others.

TASKS:
1. Fill in any known social, work, and family engagements on my calendar.
2. Decide which blocks of time are consistently open when I could volunteer either during the evenings or on the weekend.

STRATEGY 2: Contact local organizations for which I would be interested in volunteering about any opportunities.

TASKS:
1. Telephone the High Plains Food Bank.
2. Telephone the Haven of Rest Shelter.

STRATEGY 3: Make arrangements to begin volunteering on a regular schedule.

TASKS:
1. Choose the organization that matches my availability and skills.
2. Submit any paperwork required of volunteers.
3. Attend any training required for volunteers.
4. Finalize the regular schedule for my hours.

MEASURES (each month):

1. Volunteer eight hours each month to the organization.
2. Make a donation of $50 each month to the organization.

Arriving earlier in the morning than others will give you more unin-terrupted quiet time for projects. People tend to notice if you arrived before they did. You can also choose to stay later in the evening for quiet time to work. However, fewer people may notice your dedication if most lawyers, especially partners, leave before you.

If you choose to arrive early or stay late, be honest with yourself as to the reason. If it is because of uninterrupted time, then you are providing yourself with additional productivity. If it is because you are inefficient and ineffective during the normal workday, then you need to correct those time and work management issues rather than spend extra hours at the office to make up for wasted time or poor organization.

Rosemary is a hardworking lawyer in a mid-sized firm who stays later to work while it is quieter. It is not unusual for her to work until 7:30 p.m. She comes in each morning fifteen minutes before the office opens at 9:00 a.m.

At her performance evaluation, the partner comments on her lack of commitment to the firm. He touts the young male lawyers who come in at 7:00 a.m. to begin work. When she comments on her own overtime, the partner remarks that he is not there at 7:30 p.m. and cannot verify that she indeed works that late.

Taylor is a lawyer who is struggling to accomplish all the tasks during the firm's normal workday. He decides throughout the day what he wants to work on next. He is frequently rushing at the last minute to complete a project. He is constantly interrupted by colleagues' drop-in visits, telephone calls, and hundreds of e-mails. He will start on a project only to be distracted by another project on his desk. He spends a great deal of time each day hunting for files or papers that he needs. Taylor works many nights until 10:00 p.m. trying to stay on top of his workload.

Do not become the firm's "softie" who always stays late for everyone else's last-minute tasks. You need to set boundaries on demands at work and their interference with your personal life. All of us have stayed extra hours to help a colleague in an unexpected crisis. However, staying late for another person's work should not become the norm.

Think *very* carefully before you agree to work late. This is especially true if it means modifying or canceling prior plans. Agreeing will diminish your self-worth and the importance of the other people who are involved in those canceled plans. Also realize that you may legitimately decline a request even if your only reason is that you are exhausted and need to go home.

Ask yourself these questions before you agree to be the person who is imposed upon by a colleague:

- Is this person a chronic procrastinator who delays starting projects and then needs to be bailed out by someone?
- Is this person someone who is always trying to get other people to do his or her work?
- Is this person someone you owe a favor to because he or she helped you out last month?
- Does the task truly have to be done tonight, or could it be completed the next day—preferably by someone else?
- Does the task relate to expertise you already have, so you can complete it without having to first gain background or a new skill?
- Does the task relate to a client matter with which you are already familiar, so it will require no extra time to gain context?
- Can you trust the time estimate this person is giving you for completion, or does he or she always underestimate time for tasks?
- Can you complete the task in less than an hour?
- Are there other important reasons why you should agree? (Think managing partner or mega client.)

Philip is finalizing his to-do list for the next day. It is 4:45 p.m., and he is looking forward to going home after a very busy and stressful day.

At 4:50 p.m. another new associate named Roger rushes in and asks Philip to stay late with him to finish drafting a contract for the Mullins file. The project is due at 9:00 a.m. and was assigned three weeks ago. Roger did not realize how long it would take him to draft the contract. He will be at the firm all night without help. With help, he thinks they can finish by midnight. This is the third time in two months that Roger has asked for last-minute help.

Avoid using your vacation time to catch up on client matters. Instead of taking work with you, spend uninterrupted project time in the office to catch up on all files *before* you go on vacation. Your family and friends will not be amused if you spend the entire vacation working.

Include a note with instructions in each file folder for which you expect work to occur while you are gone. Have a detailed meeting before you leave with the lawyer assigned to monitor your files and any staff member who will be fielding other tasks. Leave contact details and request that they only be used if something important is needed.

Maria has packed up two boxes of files to take with her on vacation. The client matters in the files are all ones that were on the back burner but are now becoming critical. She just never gets to them during the workweek—even with overtime. There are always more-pressing matters.

Her husband, Patrick, sighs as he places the file boxes in the trunk of the car. He had hoped that this year Maria would just enjoy their time at the cabin without having to work. Although he enjoys fishing and can stay occupied while she works, he would much rather spend time with his wife.

Avoid using your personal time to catch up on reading in your practice area. Too many lawyers use weekend or vacation time for legal journals and other legal updating materials. Instead, schedule uninterrupted office time at least once every two weeks to review these materials.

Be realistic about your future with your legal employer and seek your balance accordingly. The internal politics and prospects differ with each legal employer. Do excellent work and provide your clients with top-notch service. However, do not deceive yourself about prospects in your firm or its loyalty to you. Recognize that your firm's decisions in a budget crisis will be purely bottom-line oriented and will unlikely consider all the extra overtime hours you put in or the personal goals that you sacrificed for the firm.

Your family needs to be your number one priority. Your family may include parents, siblings, a spouse, children, a significant other, or pets. Whether human or animal companions are in your life, you need to be home to provide love and attention.

The risk of divorce for lawyers is very real. You do not want to end up being your firm's highest-paid lawyer with the biggest house and fastest car but have no one to share it with after all your success.

For many lawyers, aging parents or siblings with special needs may be among their responsibilities. Lawyers often relate stories of regret for time they missed with a relative or friend because of work only to have that person die unexpectedly. No amount of success can make up for lost relationships and memories.

Matt is concerned about his marriage. As an associate, he is regularly working sixty-five hours a week and often more. He has to cancel plans with his wife at least twice a month. He has even missed several special celebrations because he forgot. If he manages to get home at some decent hour, he falls asleep on the couch watching television. Jayne tries to be supportive, but Matt knows she is frustrated. She has started accepting social engagements without him.

Matt feels he is between a rock and a hard place. How can he become a partner if he does not get the billable hours and bonuses? As he ponders the problem, he suddenly remembers a speaker during his law school orientation. The hotshot partner bragged about his important career, enormous salary, big house, and fast car. During the question-and-answer period, a first-year student asked about his family and hobbies. The partner paused, laughed, and remarked that he was on his third marriage, had no children, and did not have any hobbies.

Take care of yourself and adopt a healthy lifestyle. Sleep, nutritious meals, exercise, and relaxation are essential to both your personal and professional success. Research clearly shows that if you have a healthy lifestyle, you will be more productive on tasks, retain more information, have more energy, experience less stress, have a more positive outlook, and live longer. As a lawyer, your brain is one of your most valuable assets; protect it through your lifestyle choices.

Medical research confirms that you are chronically sleep deprived if you get less than seven hours of sleep per night regularly. Research also shows that your brain and body work better if you have a consistent sleep schedule. Go to bed at the same time Sunday through Thursday nights. Get up at the same time Monday through Friday mornings. On the weekends, vary your sleep schedule by no more than two and a half hours.

You know the drill. Avoid caffeine, sugary drinks, and fast food. Eat more fruits and vegetables. Eat lean meats and fish. Eat smaller portions. Cut back on your fat intake. Increase your good HDL and lower your bad LDL.

Try to exercise five times a week for thirty minutes. You do not need a weekly regimen of ten to fifteen hours in the gym to gain the improvements of exercise. Walking 10,000 steps a day is touted as great exercise. Fortunately, regular exercise is also one of the best stress-reduction strategies you can find.

Get in touch with your spiritual side. Research indicates that people who believe in a higher being are less stressed and live longer. You will feel less overwhelmed and less alone as you negotiate your career and life's problems.

Remember that your health is nonnegotiable. If you lose your health, you cannot get it back. Regular doctor and dental appointments are important for preventative care. If you notice changes in vision or hearing, schedule examinations.

Lawyers too often foolishly ignore warning signs only to end up with serious medical consequences. Heart palpitations, shortness of breath, dizziness, severe headaches, stomach pains, heartburn—they get ignored. Go to the doctor when something is not right. Follow the doctor's instructions. Take time off if that is what your doctor indicates is needed. No one is indispensable at work; others can cover for you.

If you have fallen into the habit of making your work everything in your life, you need to reevaluate. There is more to life than your employer, colleagues, and clients. Get out and meet other people. Take up hobbies that you enjoy. Allow your personal life to flourish as well as your professional life.

....

Reflection and Strategies

1. What are the personal values that are integral to your life and provide you with satisfaction?
2. What is one personal goal that you can focus on during several months to incorporate these personal values into your life? What strategies and tasks will help you reach that goal? How will you measure your success?
3. Consider your arrival and departure times at the office for most days. Are your choices intentional to provide uninterrupted time for projects? Or are your choices caused by inefficient and ineffective habits during the normal

workday? If the latter, what strategies can you implement for greater productivity?

4. How many times in the past month have you allowed a colleague to impose on your personal time with a last-minute crisis at the end of the day? What strategies can you implement to set realistic boundaries regarding your time?

5. How many vacation days did you use this year/last year to catch up on legal reading or client files? How many weekends or evenings did you use for the same tasks?

6. Do your family members know that they are your number one priority? Do you just tell them that, or do you actually show them that is the case?

7. Have you made your health a priority by getting enough sleep, eating nutritious meals, exercising regularly, and scheduling preventative health care? If not, why not? How can you correct any deficits in this area?

Preventing Burnout

In the best of times, the practice of law is stressful and often unforgiving on lawyers' physical, mental, and emotional health. Large numbers of lawyers leave for other employment each year rather than continue in the stressful environment of legal practice. Sadly, some lawyers turn to drugs or alcohol to deal with the stress.

The economic climate has increased practitioner stress. Equity partnerships are rarely on offer; salaried partnerships are the default for even the best associates. Some partners focus on the bottom line with minimal concern for loyalty to lawyers or even their fellow partners. Work is outsourced to save money. Firms go bankrupt, merge, or lay off lawyers with regularity. Experienced lawyers find themselves unemployed overnight. After a layoff, the remaining lawyers are expected to pick up the slack. The fear of additional layoffs adds to their already significant stress.

Burnout is a very real concern for lawyers in the best circumstances. Today, with the current conditions, it is even more likely. This chapter focuses on some ways to help you prevent burnout.

Evaluate your balance between work and personal time. For two weeks, keep track of the hours you spend in the office and the hours you have for personal time. Include your commute time as office time to gain a true picture of your remaining hours for a personal life.

There are 168 hours in a week. Subtract 49 hours off the top for a consistent sleep schedule, which is a necessity. (As mentioned previously, you should get no less than seven hours of sleep per night consistently to avoid being chronically sleep deprived. Less sleep will negatively impact your productivity, focus, and memory.) That leaves you with 119 hours of awake time.

From the 119 hours, subtract 14 hours for meals; this total is based on one hour for dinner and a half hour for breakfast and lunch each day. Skipping meals is not a good option because your brain and body need fuel. (This total will be too low if you prepare every meal yourself rather than eat meals prepared for you by family or restaurants. It will also be low if you take a longer time for meals.) You now have 105 hours left.

You will need time for dressing, bathing, and other personal care; subtract 14 hours for these personal routines. This total includes two hours a day for time to get ready in the morning, change clothes when you get home, and complete a routine before going to bed. You now have 91 hours left in your week.

Now consider your work and commute hours. If you commute an hour per day each way and work 55 hours at the office, including a partial day on the weekend, you use 67 hours for your professional life. You then have 24 hours left for your personal life. In other words, your professional life accounts for nearly three times as many hours as your personal life. For many lawyers, their professional lives consume even more than 67 hours per week.

See the calculations below on how different choices about commute time and work hours can change your personal lifestyle significantly. Lawyer A's choices were the ones we just discussed. Lawyer B chose to live closer to work to decrease commute time by half and to spend slightly fewer hours in the office over five days rather than going into the office on the weekend. Lawyer B gained 50 percent more personal time than Lawyer A's schedule allowed.

Relatively minor lifestyle changes can make major differences in your work-life balance and the likelihood of becoming burned out. Here are a few changes to consider:

- Live closer to your work to allow for a shorter commute time. Often, choosing an alternative neighborhood with a different commuter route can still provide you with the amenities you want in your price range. Sacrificing some square footage by living in a city in order to gain more personal time by not commuting may also be worth the trade-off.
- Live in a location that allows you to commute on public transportation, by train, or by van pool to lower the stress of traffic jams.
- Change your commute time to avoid high-traffic times. Even ten or fifteen minutes may take advantage of a window of time with fewer cars on the road.

Lifestyle Choices of Two Lawyers: Commute Time and Office Hours

Lawyer A	Lawyer B
168 hours a week	168 hours a week
−49 hours sleep	−49 hours sleep
119 hours	119 hours
−14 hours meals	−14 hours meals
105 hours	105 hours
−14 hours personal care	−14 hours personal care
91 hours	91 hours
−12 hours commute (6 days x 2 hours)	−5 hours commute (5 days x 1 hour)
79 hours	86 hours
−55 hours in the office (6 days)	−50 hours in the office (5 days)
24 hours personal time	**36 hours personal time**

- Arrive early or stay late to have uninterrupted work time and increased productivity during the week in order to avoid having to work on the weekend.
- If your firm allows for flexible hours, arrive and correspondingly leave early or late to avoid traffic and decrease your commuting time.
- If your firm allows lawyers to work from home, choose to do so several days a week to decrease your commuting time.

Evaluate your progress on your personal goals. Ask yourself the following questions:

- Does the time left for your personal life each week provide you with the rest and relaxation that you need?
- Does your current situation allow you to spend time on the activities and with the people you value most?

- Do you have enough energy after your workweek to pursue activities for your own enjoyment?
- Does your current lifestyle allow you the time away from the office to meet the personal goals you set in Chapter 13?

If you answered no to any of these questions, you need to decrease your hours in the office before you become completely burned out and disconnected from things that are important to you personally.

Consider how you can change your environment, time commitment, or duties at work to expand time for your personal goals. Choose two strategies you will implement this month to increase your personal time and begin to meet your personal goals.

Review your projects and priorities at work. Ask yourself some additional questions:

- Are the projects and priorities that you have chosen realistic?
- Are you trying to accomplish too much too soon?
- Are you working on projects and priorities for others that you have no control over and, therefore, are feeling overwhelmed?
- Are you wasting time on the unimportant tasks instead of focusing on the most important work?

You want to focus on the right projects to get the payoff you need and the billable hours your firm expects. Proportion your work and time to get the most results.

Evaluate your time and work management skills. It is time for a few more questions:

- Are you being as efficient and effective as you can be?
- Do you need to set aside more uninterrupted project time?
- Do you need to delegate work to others?
- Do you need to ask for more staff support than you currently have?
- Do you need to "just say no" to additional work demands?

Review the prior chapters in this book and decide which strategies you need to implement to become more productive by using your time more wisely and getting more results from your time. Staff members with whom you work regularly may be able to make suggestions. Ask colleagues who seem to be very efficient and effective to share their time and work management tips.

Evaluate options you may have at your firm to provide more personal time to avoid burnout. Over the last two decades, some law firms have implemented variations to the traditional lawyer lifestyle to provide more work-life balance. If your firm provides options, you may want to trade the high salary and stress for an alternative work arrangement:

- Telecommuting: The ease of technology means that lawyers can work anywhere and be highly productive. Law firms have adjusted to the reality that lawyers who travel regularly can work effectively and efficiently through today's technology. Telecommuting several days a week can be a boon to your family life whether you want more time with your spouse, are caring for children or elderly parents, or just want to avoid the commute.
- Going off partner track: More law firms offer positions now to retain high-quality lawyers with good billable hours who do not want to compete for the few partner slots that may open. With lower salaries and reduced billable hours, these lawyers opt for more personal time and less stress. You may need to tighten your financial belt with this option, but the trade-off can be worth it in peace of mind and lifestyle.
- Going part-time: Although this trend started with women lawyers, both women and men now make the choice. They opt for part-time work so they can have more flexibility and personal time. They decide that the financial and promotional sacrifices are worth it to have a lifestyle that allows them "to have it all" without giving up personal life choices for a law career.

These options need to be weighed carefully in light of the culture and financial stability of your firm. Some lawyers fear that they will be easier targets during a layoff if they work differently than their colleagues even though they produce equal quality work. In some cases, the bottom line might actually favor the part-time or non-partner-track lawyer who is less expensive to retain. You need to understand your firm's dynamics and decision-making process when considering these options.

Consider whether switching to a different practice area within your firm would provide you with a better lifestyle and avoid burnout. The practice area that you loved initially may no longer provide the same satisfaction or match your current family priorities and responsibilities. Another specialty may demand less travel, fewer late nights preparing for trial, or less emotional wear and tear. Consider whether you could switch from commercial litigation to corporate work, general civil litigation to employment law, or child abuse and neglect cases to other family matters.

Consider whether a switch in employer would provide you with the lifestyle you want. Lateral hires have become common in today's legal market. You may want to switch to another law firm similar in size to yours but with a very different firm culture. Alternatively, you may desire to switch to a small or mid-sized firm where the personal benefits will outweigh a potentially lower salary. It is not unusual for lawyers to leave private practice for in-house counsel or government agency positions after a few years. Some highly credentialed lawyers with adjunct teaching experience or published articles will switch to law school or business school teaching positions. Other lawyers will switch to legal clinics, career services, development, academic support, or other positions at law schools. Explore your options through networking. Seek out a change *before* you become burned out.

Evaluate whether you are on the road to burnout. Lawyers, by the very characteristics of their profession, are intelligent, motivated by challenges, hardworking, persistent, and focused on solutions. They can become so focused on a win or the price tag on a deal that they lose sight of the world around them.

Ask yourself the following questions to determine whether you have become too consumed with work and are heading for burnout:

- Have you become driven by the outcome rather than a love of the law?
- Have you become focused on work to the exclusion of everything else?
- Are you traveling so regularly for work that you have to remind yourself what city you are in or when you were last at your apartment for a full week?
- Do you cancel or forget a commitment to your family several times a month?
- Does your child know not to expect you at the football game or dance recital you said you would attend?
- Does your spouse know that your staff member ordered her birthday flowers or a gift instead of you?
- Did you spend a large portion of the last family vacation talking to clients on the telephone, answering e-mails, or working on client files?
- Have you become addicted to your smartphone or tablet?
- Have you become an adrenaline junkie who cannot live without the next big deal or court battle?
- Do you either avoid exercise because you have no time or overdose on exercise to release accumulated stress?
- Do you have headaches, heartburn, stomach pains, shortness of breath, or other medical symptoms regularly?
- Have you become irritable, depressed, anxious, or unfocused lately?
- Do you either have regular insomnia or sleep constantly when you are home?

If you have become obsessed with work, you are well on the way to burnout. You need to readjust your attitude to discover the world around you and the family waiting in the wings for you to notice them.

Talk to your physician or a counselor if you need assistance in choosing lifestyle options to avoid burnout.

Reflection and Strategies

1. Evaluate your week to see how many hours you spend for work/commuting and how many hours you reserve for personal time.
2. If your evaluation indicates fewer hours for personal time than you want each week, what lifestyle changes can you make relatively easily to correct the balance?
3. What options are available at your legal employer to gain more work-life balance: telecommuting, part-time work, going off partner track, switching specialties? Which of these options might be successfully applied to your circumstances?
4. Which time and work management strategies could you implement to prevent burnout and gain more work-life balance? Prioritize those strategies and schedule their implementation.
5. Use the questions in the chapter to evaluate whether you are on the road to burnout, and seek assistance now before you reach that point.

Appendix A: Quick Tips for Better Time and Work Management

The main chapters of this book include far more suggestions than are in this appendix. Most of the quick tips here are discussed in much greater detail within the chapters. There are some additional tips here to supplement the main text.

Asking for Assistance

1. Before asking for assistance from others, carefully evaluate what assistance you need so you can express your specific need succinctly.
2. Become astute as to the people who sincerely want to help by observing people's work.
3. Do not consider it a weakness to ask for help, because asking for help is more efficient and effective than struggling or doing the assignment incorrectly.

Billing Units

1. Record billing units at the time the work is completed so your bill will be accurate and you will not overlook any billing units.
2. Record sufficient details about the work at the same time so you can produce an informative invoice, which will be less likely to be disputed by the client.
3. Record all your time and allow your supervisor to determine what amount will ultimately be billed to the client.
4. Become more efficient and effective in your work methods if your actual time on tasks consistently exceeds what your firm can bill the client.
5. Avoid doing work that is more appropriately done by a lower-fee staff member so you will not lose time elsewhere that you could have billed at the higher lawyer rate.
6. Capture all your billable units when you are out of the office with a smartphone application, a VPN connection to your firm's computer system, or by manually writing them down.

Burnout Prevention

1. Keep track for two weeks to see how much time you spend at work versus how much time you have for personal matters.
2. Evaluate your progress on your personal goals in light of what you found out in your tracking.
3. Consider lifestyle changes that can improve your quality of life by minimizing your commute and allowing more personal time: move closer to work, pick an alternate commuter route, use public transportation, arrive early or stay late if your firm has flexible hours, telecommute several days a week.
4. Evaluate your time and work management skills and implement new strategies to make you more productive at the office during the week so you can spend less time there on the weekend.
5. If your firm provides options for work hours or tracks, consider whether those options would improve your lifestyle: flexible arrival/departure times, telecommuting, going off the partner track, or going part-time.
6. Consider whether changing your practice area would provide you with a better lifestyle and prevent burnout.
7. Consider whether switching to a different legal employer would provide you with a better lifestyle and prevent burnout.
8. Schedule time with your spouse or significant other, friends, children, extended family, and pets and stick to those commitments.
9. Schedule exercise for at least thirty minutes five times a week and stick to your schedule.
10. Get at least seven hours of sleep per night to be more alert and productive and improve your memory.
11. Take short breaks throughout your workday to increase your focus and energy.
12. Take a lunch break away from your desk for at least 30 minutes.

Client Files

1. Realize that your organization of client files will vary with the paperless/less paper status of your firm.

2. Keep only the client files that you are using for the day on your work surfaces.

3. Avoid stacking files around the room if you do not have enough file cabinets, because the files can easily be knocked over and papers scattered.

4. For extra file space for client files that you use regularly, use brightly colored banker's boxes or plastic storage boxes to sort the files by priority of the work, court or client deadlines, practice area, type of project, or client.

5. When interrupted while working on a client file, always make notes and place them in the file to indicate where you were and the next several things to accomplish.

6. Spring clip miscellaneous reminders, telephone messages, and small notes for a client's file together; at the end of the day, photocopy any unfinished items onto a sheet of paper so that you are less likely to misplace the information.

Competing Demands

1. Create a project list to track all your assignments and include the date assigned, person assigning, type of assignment, client details, deadlines, comments, assigning lawyer contact preferences, any additional instructions, and completion date.

2. Confirm complex assignments and deadlines in writing whenever possible.

3. Check your project list for conflicting deadlines for the final work product or any intermediate tasks.

4. Alert the assigning lawyer immediately if there is a problem with conflicting deadlines or meeting a deadline because of unexpected delays.

5. Estimate the time you will need for each task within your overall project and total the amount of time you will need for the entire project.

6. If you are not good at estimating time, estimate a range of time for a task and take the higher number in the range and add 20 percent to it.

7. Set an artificial deadline at least two days before the actual deadline to allow yourself time for a final edit, format changes, or correction of unforeseen problems.
8. If you have multiple projects due on the same date, stagger your artificial deadlines: one two days earlier, one four days earlier, and so forth.
9. Use a dry-erase wall calendar or project management software so you can lay out your tasks for multiple projects that you are completing concurrently. If using a dry-erase calendar, be careful of confidentiality when posting it.
10. When you are given an assignment without a fixed deadline, do not wait to begin the tasks related to it; instead plan where you will fit the tasks in with your other assignments.
11. Know when you can work on multiple projects simultaneously and when you need to do them sequentially because of their complexity.
12. If you have conflicting deadlines from multiple lawyers, get input from your supervisor to resolve what your priorities should be.

Crises

1. When a crisis occurs, pause rather than immediately react, and take a few minutes to plan your response. If you need to take a short break to handle the stress, walk within the building or do some deep-breathing exercises.
2. By listing all the specific tasks that must be completed, estimating the time that each task will take, and listing any staff or colleagues who can help you with the tasks, you will gain control over the situation.
3. Consult your daily task list and calendar and determine which tasks and appointments can be rescheduled and which can be delegated.
4. In a crisis, consider whether you have the authority to make the decisions on delaying or reassigning tasks and, if not, consult with someone more senior.

Deadlines and Important Dates

1. Duplicate your calendar on all your electronic tools for easy access: smartphone, tablet, laptop.
2. Have a backup for electronic calendaring, such as a hard-copy daily planner, in case there is a computer system problem.
3. If you work on large projects, consider using a dry-erase, month- or year-at-a-glance wall calendar or project management software to track multiple tasks and deadlines.
4. No calendaring method will assist you if you do not look at it regularly.

Delegation

1. Be honest with yourself about whether you resist delegation when you actually need assistance.
2. Realize that there are three categories of tasks that can potentially be delegated: tasks you do not like doing, tasks that someone else is better at doing, and specific tasks within a larger project.
3. When you delegate tasks, always provide clear, detailed, and accurate instructions and a clear deadline.
4. When you delegate tasks, provide written instructions as well as discussion for complex tasks and then check back later with the staff person to answer questions.
5. Choose very carefully the people to whom you delegate, and consider each person's skills, talents, and abilities.
6. As early as possible, delegate tasks that are not dependent on other steps in the project being completed first.
7. Set an artificial deadline for the staff member at least two days before your actual deadline so that you will have time to integrate the work into the overall project or to make adjustments to the final work product.
8. Use a project delegation chart to track any delegated tasks; include the task description, the date you delegated the task, the person's name, the tasks assigned, work products required, any deadlines, and any other comments.

9. If the person to whom you want to delegate work is not a staff member who reports directly to you, get permission from that person's supervisor to assign the work.

10. If you and several colleagues share the staff member to whom you want to delegate a major project, it is polite to give your colleagues a heads-up that the person will be busy on a project for you during a certain time period.

11. As appropriate to the tasks delegated, check on the staff member at several points to see if questions or problems have arisen, but do not micromanage the task.

12. Review the returned work product immediately so that any problem areas can be resolved quickly.

13. If the quality of the returned work product is unacceptable, determine what is needed to rectify the situation and request assistance as needed.

14. Be sure to thank the staff member for good work after the project is over and give constructive feedback if appropriate.

15. After a delegated project, evaluate your performance as a delegator (choice of person, timing of the delegation, instructions, follow-up) and decide how you could be more effective as a delegator in the future.

Document Assembly

1. Use subscription document assembly software to draft documents whenever possible.

2. If subscription software is unavailable, make your own templates for the documents you draft most often.

3. Make templates for common letters that you write: client engagement, nonacceptance of a client, follow-up letters, etc.

4. Make sure when using a template that you save your new version separately and do not copy over the original version or change word processing settings in the original template.

5. Always carefully check your document to make sure you have not left other clients' names or information from prior versions in the current document.

E-mail

1. Determine whether a face-to-face discussion, e-mail, or telephone conversation is more appropriate for the information that you need to relay.
2. Do not hit "reply all" unless everyone needs to know your reply.
3. Avoid emoticons and text acronyms in your e-mail messages.
4. Do not use all caps in an e-mail because it is the equivalent of shouting at the other person.
5. Never hit "send" when you have typed an angry, sarcastic, or otherwise emotional e-mail.
6. Do not send anything by e-mail that you are not willing to let your grandmother see.
7. Only send an e-mail if immediacy is needed, and then only send the e-mail to the people who really need to receive it.
8. Consider any ethical or other problems that may result from sending an e-mail.
9. Think before you write, and write formally with correct sentence structure, word choice, grammar, punctuation, and spelling.
10. Keep your e-mail within one screen in length if possible and use an attachment if an e-mail will be longer.
11. Always include a subject line that imparts the important information about the e-mail.
12. Include any deadline and requested action in the subject line and at the beginning of the e-mail.
13. Only flag an e-mail as high importance if it really is and needs to be answered quickly.
14. Avoid the unnecessary "thank you" and "you're welcome" e-mails.
15. Decrease e-mail distractions by turning down the volume of the alert, shortening the time of the new message alert window, minimizing your inbox screen, or temporarily turning off the alerts.
16. If possible, do not look at e-mails while you need to concentrate on projects.
17. If you must check e-mail every half hour or hour, respond to only urgent e-mails before you go back to your project.

18. Avoid clutter in your inbox by using the rule function to send listserv, subscription service, and RSS feed e-mails automatically to inbox folders.
19. If possible, determine an action for an e-mail the first time you look at it: reply, forward, delegate, file, or delete.
20. Set up archive file folders on a different drive if possible, so the archive folders will not count toward your inbox space quota.
21. Take five minutes mid-morning, mid-afternoon, and before the end of the day to review your inbox for any overlooked items.
22. Use the e-mail tools for your e-mail provider to help you manage your inbox: sort, rules, flags, categories, filters, etc.
23. Minimize clutter in your e-mail archive files by spending at least a few minutes once a month to delete unwanted e-mails or folders.

Equipment

1. Keep your office stocked with your essential supplies so that you do not waste time looking for a legal pad, highlighters, paper clips, or staples.
2. Dictate rather than word process to speed drafting—most lawyers dictate faster than they type once they become accustomed to dictation.
3. Use a digital voice recorder to capture your thoughts and draft documents when out of the office.
4. Use speech recognition software to save time in drafting documents if you prefer to see the words on the screen while you dictate.
5. Investigate applications (apps) for your smartphone to track time and expenses for client billing, provide dictation capabilities, manage task lists, and access legal reference materials.
6. Learn how to use the photocopier, scanner, or other equipment in case you have no one to help you when you arrive early or stay late.
7. Purchase secure, locking file cabinets and a fireproof safe for your solo practice. Lock both each night, and choose carefully who will have the keys and combination.

General Points

1. You need to be both efficient (use time wisely) and effective (get the most results from the time) if you are to excel at time and work management.
2. You must make time to get things done; you will never just find time.
3. Implement new time and work management strategies in stages by adding new strategies as others become a natural part of your workday.
4. Set reasonable boundaries on your time because you cannot be all things to all people.
5. Have a plan to deal with the unexpected so you are not overwhelmed.
6. Evaluate your legal environment so that you can wisely choose strategies and modify them for your specific work situation.

Goal Setting

1. Choose a maximum of ten professional goals for the coming year that are realistic, manageable, specific, and measurable.
2. Pick several goals that will make you more valuable to your employer and improve your future career prospects.
3. Pick several goals that will make you more efficient in your job so that you use your time more wisely.
4. Pick several goals that will make you more effective in your job so that you get greater results out of the time you spend.
5. List strategies for implementing each of your goals during the year and include specific tasks for each strategy.
6. Review your goals monthly to evaluate your progress and brainstorm new strategies if necessary to make the goals more achievable.

Incoming and Outgoing Items

1. Sort your incoming desk stack and make decisions about the items in the stack at least three times a day: morning, midday, and before going home.

2. Sort incoming items into seven categories: file (client file or reference file), forward (for another's information), do (easily handled items), delegate (for another's action), schedule (listed for later action), read (update information), and trash (not needed).
3. Only keep items that you truly need; if the information is online or someone else in the firm tracks the information, consider not keeping a duplicate copy.
4. If a task can be done in fifteen minutes or less, take care of it immediately if you have the time available.
5. Add any items that you need to do later to your appropriate task list (master, monthly, weekly, or daily) and calendar any deadlines related to the items.
6. If a subscription or routed item is no longer of interest, cancel the subscription or remove your name from the routing process.
7. Use a tickler file system (file folders for each month and the dates for the current month) to supplement your incoming sort process and place papers that are needed for future tasks in the appropriate month or date file.
8. Write down small, miscellaneous tasks (a question to ask your staff member, a name and telephone number to call, a reminder to e-mail someone) on a stenographer's (steno) spiral pad and check off the item when completed.
9. Alternatively, use electronic sticky notes and electronic task lists to track these miscellaneous items.

Meetings – Chairpersons

1. Invite only the people whose attendance is really necessary.
2. Provide a meeting agenda and any pertinent documents ahead of time so that participants can think about the topics and review any materials.
3. Start the meeting on time so others know that they need to show up on time.
4. Keep the discussion on track throughout the meeting and ask focused questions if the group starts to get off topic.

5. Do not move on to another agenda item until the current item is discussed fully, acted upon, or tabled for future discussion.
6. Have a basic familiarity with *Robert's Rules of Order* to keep the committee procedures organized.
7. Summarize at the very end of the meeting any assignments that have been given or outstanding matters that members need to consider before the next meeting.
8. End the meeting within an hour if possible.
9. If a committee will meet regularly, try to schedule the meetings for the same time and day on whatever regular rotation is appropriate.

Meetings – Committee Members

1. Never enter a meeting without a laptop or pad and pen to take notes and always have any documents or other materials you will need.
2. Always arrive on time for the meetings and preferably a few minutes early so that you will be ready and focused by the start of the meeting.
3. Complete any assigned tasks before the meeting and be prepared to give a concise and organized summary/presentation to the group.
4. Keep your comments on topic and concise and ask only relevant questions.
5. Do not work on other items (reviewing client letters, reading articles, reading e-mail, texting) while you are in the meeting.
6. Stay for the entire meeting and do not gather your belongings to leave until the meeting is adjourned.

Miscellany

1. Leave windows of time on your calendar for travel time to and from appointments, meetings, or court.
2. Block off regular times on your calendar each day for returning phone calls, responding to e-mails, and being available to staff.

3. Save steps and time by accomplishing in one trip all errands within the building that are related to the same floor, destination, or colleague.
4. When someone stops you in the hallway, suggest they walk with you to your intended destination so you can avoid being late for your next appointment.
5. When a colleague leaves a message that he needs to talk with you, go to the colleague's office in order to have more control over the timing and length of the meeting.
6. When someone drops by and asks if you have a minute to talk, state the time frame you can spare and then stick to it: "I am working on a deadline, but I can give you ten minutes."
7. If your employer does not provide them, develop template forms for any routine administrative items that you complete: requesting supplies, routing items to others, instructions to your support staff.
8. If you get far behind in your work, prioritize the projects, break each project into a series of small tasks, and ask for assistance on tasks that can be delegated.

Procrastination

1. Getting started is the hardest part; once you make a start, no matter how small, you are likely to continue working on the task.
2. Complete several small preparation tasks to get you into the mood for working.
3. Break down assignments into smaller task components that will seem less daunting and also get completed and crossed off your task list more quickly—two positive incentives.
4. If you still procrastinate on the smaller tasks, break the task down even further so that you cannot justify delaying: "I'll read one page" or "I'll write just the first interrogatory."
5. Set interim reporting deadlines with your supervisor to discuss your project so you are accountable to someone for your progress.

6. Determine a rewards system, with the size of the reward linked to the size of the task completed (a cup of coffee, a fifteen-minute discussion about last night's NFL game, lunch at your favorite restaurant).

Productivity

1. Track your energy levels for two weeks, noting when you have the most energy and are most productive and when you have the least energy and are least productive.
2. Schedule your most challenging tasks for high-energy times; use low-energy times for routine tasks.
3. If you have a consistent pattern of high-energy times, schedule uninterrupted project time during those periods several days a week.
4. Track for one week where you are losing time because of interruptions and analyze the amount of time lost and the main causes.
5. Take five-minute breaks every sixty to ninety minutes during the day to revitalize your brain cells.
6. Get up and move around on your breaks rather than check e-mail.
7. To be more productive in the afternoon, take your lunch break but opt for healthy foods rather than heavy meals that will make you lethargic and sleepy.

Project Time

1. Schedule project work during your high-energy times whenever possible.
2. If your project time is consistent every week, it will be easier for others to anticipate and honor your request for uninterrupted project time.
3. If your firm culture allows it, close your door when working on a project.
4. If possible, have someone else field your telephone calls and e-mails during your project time.

5. Give your staff member a list of people who have permission to interrupt your project time *at any time* (certain clients, your supervisor, your family) and those people who *temporarily* can interrupt your project time (the client you have been playing telephone tag with, opposing counsel on a specific case).

Research

1. If you have multiple research projects, take time to prioritize them and carefully plan how you will meet the multiple deadlines.
2. Complex projects may need to be worked on one at a time, whereas less complex research can be juggled concurrently.
3. Take time to think through the parameters of your assignment and note any specific instructions that are important to your success on the project.
4. Determine your current expertise in the research topic and consider what background knowledge you will need before you begin your actual billable research.
5. Plan which sources and search terms will be beneficial and prioritize your research steps.
6. Track your research carefully: all sources checked and all search terms used.
7. Periodically pause and evaluate your research progress: sources you have found, gaps in your research, dead ends, and issues completed.
8. Periodically, also take time to brief the cases, summarize the relevant statutes, and organize your research into a skeleton outline to determine how you will use the materials.
9. Ask your assigning lawyer whether you need to pursue side issues that you have discovered; it will be difficult to re-create your research thread if you initially ignore a relevant side issue.
10. Remember to update all your sources and follow up on any subsequent history that impacts your research.
11. Make sure that you know your firm's policies on electronic research because you may not have as extensive access as you did in law school or at your last firm.

12. Get to know the law librarians because they can help you become more efficient and effective in your research.
13. Keep your legal research books from law school in your desk drawer to check background information on a particular hard-copy resource or type of research with which you are less familiar.
14. Keep your bar review outlines in your desk drawer for a quick refresher in an area of law that you have not thought about for a while.

Reserved and Windfall Times

1. Schedule several blocks of reserved time on your calendar each week that are kept clear to allow you some flexibility in your schedule for when unexpected events occur during your week.
2. Use reserved time for unexpected projects, rescheduling of tasks or appointments because of a crisis, extra time needed if you misjudged how long a project would take, or new appointments requested on short notice.
3. If a block of reserved time is not needed for something unexpected, use the time to get ahead on another project or complete administrative tasks.
4. Take advantage of windfall time that occurs when another task takes less time than scheduled, a meeting gets canceled, or a block of time opens in your schedule for some other reason.
5. Use fifteen or less windfall minutes to check your e-mail, straighten up your desk, reprioritize your task lists, review and sign routine letters, compose several routine e-mails, or make a short telephone call.
6. Use twenty to thirty windfall minutes to review the subsequent history for several cases, check citations in a legal memorandum, compose a short letter to your client, read an article in your reading stack, make a longer telephone call, compose a longer e-mail, visit with a staff member to review progress on a project, or complete a partial sort of your incoming stack.
7. Use forty-five to sixty windfall minutes to prepare for an upcoming meeting, read and brief several judicial opinions for a research

project, compose a lengthy client letter, work on an outline for a legal memorandum, edit a document, read multiple articles in your reading stack, or sort your entire incoming stack.

Smartphones

1. If Big Law issued you a smartphone, you are expected to be available; check your messages regularly.
2. It is rude to check your smartphone or reply to text messages when you are in a meeting, interviewing a client, or talking with another lawyer.
3. Texting under the table is still rude when you are in any of these situations.
4. Be on your best behavior in court because judges do not take kindly to technology interruptions.
5. Pick an appropriate ringtone for a professional environment.

Social Media

1. Do not allow the informality of social media to lure you into forgetting your professional role as a lawyer.
2. Consider professionalism rules carefully before you post anything: disclaimers, attorney-client privilege, potential lawyer-client relationships, conflicts of interest, advertising rules, firm policies.
3. Monitor comments to your blog and responses to your tweets to avoid content that might be inappropriate or violate professionalism rules.
4. Do not post anything about current or past cases to avoid inadvertently divulging confidential information.
5. Make sure you know how to use the privacy settings, and keep yourself updated on changes to those settings.
6. Make sure your staff members and clients also know how to use social media responsibly.

Staff Relations

1. Treat all staff with respect and collegiality.
2. Remember to say "please" and "thank you" when asking for and receiving help.

3. Take the time to learn staff members' names and how to pronounce them correctly.
4. Recognize staff members' strengths and weaknesses.
5. Know your own weaknesses and determine how staff members can assist you in those areas.
6. Discuss your priorities for the day each morning with your assigned staff members so they will know your agenda and how their own assignments correlate with your tasks.
7. Make your expectations clear because staff members cannot read your mind.
8. Realize that staff members may know more than you do about certain tasks, firm procedures, and firm politics.
9. Ask your assigned staff members how you can be more effective and efficient in your own work and coordinate your work better with them.
10. Reward your staff members with praise for quality work.
11. Discuss privately with staff members any problem areas in their work.

Task Priorities

1. Make a master list of future tasks that are important to remember.
2. Make a list of tasks to complete during the current month, including tasks from your master list, tasks related to your goals and strategies, and any new items for the month.
3. Make a weekly list of tasks for the upcoming week before you go home for the weekend, including tasks from your monthly list as well as any new items for the week.
4. Make a daily list of tasks that need to be completed the next day before you go home in the evening, including tasks from your weekly list as well as any new items for the day.
5. Prioritize the items on your weekly and daily task lists into three categories: *most important*, *important*, and *least important*.
6. Realize the difference between real and perceived crises and handle the first category immediately before other tasks; delay the second type for the appropriate place within your priorities for the day.

7. Work through all tasks in order of priority and only move on to a lower-priority task if you become stalled on a higher-priority task while waiting for more information or staff assistance.

8. Estimate the amount of time a task will take and complete the task within that designated block rather than allowing it to bleed into the next task's time on your calendar.

9. If you are poor at estimating time for tasks, estimate a range of time, select the higher number in the range, and add 20 percent to it.

10. Use the alarm function and the fifteen- or five-minute warnings on your smartphone or computer to track your task time.

11. Consult your task list four times a day and reevaluate whether anything has changed in your priorities or if tasks need to be added or deleted: first thing in the morning, at mid-morning, at lunch time, and at mid-afternoon.

12. Make sure that all meetings, client commitments, and deadlines are scheduled on your calendar and consider any tasks that must be completed before those scheduled events.

13. Mark completed tasks off your daily list with a yellow highlighter if the growing sea of color down the page will be more satisfying than mere ink cross-outs.

Telephone Calls

1. Determine whether a face-to-face discussion, e-mail, or telephone conversation is more appropriate for the information that you need to relay.

2. Focus on the person with whom you are meeting and avoid taking telephone calls when you have someone in your office.

3. If you must take a telephone call when someone is with you, apologize for the interruption and, if the call is confidential, ask the person to wait in the reception area.

4. Initiate your own telephone calls at times when you can focus on the conversations without rushing or being interrupted.

5. Prioritize your own telephone calls by the importance of the matter, the amount of time you have, when you need the information you are seeking, and when your client is available.

6. Plan your telephone conversation before you call and make notes to guide you if necessary.

7. Be aware of any confidentiality concerns your client has about leaving messages and plan the message you might need to leave before you call.

8. Be concise but thorough in your telephone message, enunciate, and state your name and telephone number at both the beginning and end of the message.

9. Telephone your clients regularly to avoid complaints from them that you have not kept them apprised of the status of their cases.

10. Find a balance between being responsive to your clients and getting your work done.

11. Discuss with your staff member how you want your calls handled and what information you want in telephone messages.

12. Designate at least three times during the day (mid-morning, mid-afternoon, and before the close of business) when you will always return telephone messages so that staff members who field telephone calls when you are unavailable can tell clients when to expect your return call.

13. Always return telephone calls even if you have nothing new to tell the client.

14. Leave a message if you miss the person whose call you are returning and make yourself a note of the date and time in case you need later verification.

15. If you cannot reach the person whose call you are returning after several attempts, consider e-mailing as a follow-up.

16. Short-circuit telephone tag by leaving a message detailing the specific question you have or the information the caller needs.

Travel

1. Determine whether business travel can be effectively avoided by using videoconferencing options for real-time meetings or if an in-person meeting is more appropriate.

2. Make sure your staff members have everything they need before you leave: your itinerary and contact information, access to your calendar, instructions for tasks they need to complete, and knowledge of actions that may be needed on client files.

3. Have set times each day when you will telephone a staff member to answer questions and pick up messages that cannot easily be handled through text, e-mail, or voicemail.
4. Have set times each day when you reply to e-mails and return telephone calls so that staff members will be able to tell clients when to expect to hear from you while you are traveling.
5. Use care in hotels, in airports, and at client sites to protect confidentiality so no one will overhear your telephone conversation, see your laptop screen, or read documents you are using.
6. Use your firm's travel consultant to make business travel arrangements whenever possible so that the firm will pay for the arrangements directly.
7. Use an employer's credit card if possible rather than your personal credit card for travel-related expenses.
8. If you must use your own personal credit card, have one credit card that is solely for business to make it easy to track expenses that must be reimbursed.
9. Remember to be conscientious about tracking your billing units while gone.
10. If you travel frequently, have a checklist for everything that you typically need to take with you.
11. If you travel frequently, designate a briefcase and a suitcase for business travel only and prestock them with the basics so you will just need to add clothes and a few other essentials.
12. Have a list of names and telephone numbers for all the people and services that handle personal items for you while you travel, and have preprinted instructions for these same people explaining childcare, pet care, plant care, emergency numbers, and other matters.

Work-Life Balance

1. Make a list of personal values that are important to you and refocus your professional and personal lives on integrating those values on a daily basis.

2. Set personal goals in addition to your professional goals and plan strategies and tasks for achieving them during the coming year.
3. Decline last-minute assignments that interfere with your evening or weekend plans unless it is a real emergency or there is some other compelling reason.
4. Decline diplomatically any assignments for which you do not have time because of other projects or for which you do not have the expertise—it is always better to say no than to miss a deadline or the desired standard.
5. Take your vacation every year and avoid using your vacation time to catch up on work from the office by taking files with you.
6. Do not go into the office when you are sick; you will just infect everyone else or set yourself up for a relapse.
7. Take care of yourself and adopt a healthy lifestyle with a proper diet, exercise, and sleep.
8. Make your family a priority and do not allow your professional life to jeopardize those relationships and commitments.
9. Remember that your health is nonnegotiable.

Workspace Organization

1. Arrange your office furniture so that your back or side is to the door to minimize hallway distractions.
2. Gather all the relevant materials (documents, files, books) and office supplies or tools before you begin your task to optimize your organization.
3. Keep a large area in the center of your desk clear as an *all-clear zone* and work on only one project at a time in that workspace.
4. To the left of the all-clear zone, place prioritized *to-do stacks* of work to be completed during the day.
5. At the top of the all-clear zone, place four stacks: *incoming* items such as mail or memoranda, *outgoing* items to be mailed or distributed, items to *refer to* during the day, and items for *meetings* or appointments.
6. Keep only the items that you use regularly on your work surfaces and place all other items in drawers or filing cabinets.

7. Straighten your work surfaces several times a day and put items away that are no longer needed.

8. Before leaving for the evening, clean up your work area by returning all tools and papers/files to their proper areas and lay out your prioritized to-do stacks and refer-to stack for the next day.

9. For information on workspace ergonomics, go to the Occupational Safety and Health Administration (OSHA) website: http://www.osha.gov/SLTC/etools/computerworkstations/index.html.

Writing and Editing

1. Realize that prewriting is an important step in your writing process and allows you time to mull over ideas, consider arguments for both sides, and contemplate organizational alternatives.

2. Review all your case briefs and statute summaries again and review the full-text sources to make sure that you did not miss anything important.

3. Look at the skeleton outline that you made during the research phase and evaluate it carefully to reorganize it and fill in any gaps.

4. Determine whether any sources should be used in different sections, used in multiple sections, or deleted entirely.

5. Choose which section will give you an easier entry point into the document and write that section first.

6. Do not try to write a perfect draft the first time, but instead get words on the paper and then revise.

7. If you are interrupted, make careful notes for yourself on your train of thought and the next task for completion.

8. When you return later, take time to regain your context by rereading the last section you wrote.

9. If you have written sections of your document out of order, read the sections in the correct order and rewrite as necessary to form an integrated whole.

10. Allow sufficient time for editing in multiple stages rather than editing for everything at once: correct usage of cases, statutory language and interpretation, logic of analysis in each section and in the overall document, clarity, wordiness and repetition, transitions, grammar, punctuation, citations, and format.
11. If possible, meet with your assigning lawyer after your project has been reviewed to get constructive feedback.

Appendix B:
Time-Saving and Organizational
Tips for Your Home

By becoming more organized and using your time better on home tasks, you can lower your stress during your workweek and acquire more personal time.

Bills and Papers

1. Always put bills that need to be paid in one place so that they will not be overlooked, and stack them in order of the date you need to pay them, with the earliest on top.
2. If you can afford to pay your bills as soon as they arrive, do so because you will be less likely to forget a payment or have a late payment.
3. If you can afford to have your bills paid by automatic bank draft each month, use that convenience for the same reasons.
4. Keep receipts in one place to check against your bank account and credit card statements when they arrive.
5. Once you know that all entries and charges are correct, you can discard receipts unless you need them for taxes, warranties, or purchase records.
6. For tax purposes, keep a brightly colored accordion file with categories and sort receipts and statements as you receive them.
7. If you use electronic tax preparation software, enter items as you get them throughout the year.
8. Have labeled file folders or binders in which you keep all important papers that are not related to taxes: medical test results, home warranty contract, contract of employment, etc.
9. Shred regularly any confidential papers that you no longer need.

Chores

1. If other family members are available to help, assign age-appropriate tasks to each person.

2. Determine which chores are wiser to pay a service to do than using your own time: cleaning, lawn care, dog walking, grocery delivery, errands.
3. Do a whirling-dervish cleaning twice a month so that you can just spot clean during the rest of the month.
4. Each time you do this cleaning, look for any minor repairs or preventative maintenance to be done.
5. Twice a year, do a deep cleaning of all surfaces in your home or apartment.
6. Once a month, walk around the exterior of your home and look for any repairs or preventative maintenance to be completed.
7. Schedule on a yearly calendar all the repetitive tasks that need to be done on a regular basis: change furnace filters, add water softener pellets, replace smoke detector batteries.
8. If you have difficulty being at home to have work done on your house, consider hiring a stay-at-home neighbor or retired person from church to be at your house to meet the repairman and supervise the work while you are available by telephone for questions.
9. Keep a binder for your home that includes manuals for household appliances, the major repairs done on the house, and names/numbers of service providers.

Errands

1. Save gas and time by planning personal errands and your route: run errands in the same part of town together, and group errands by when they need to be accomplished.
2. Have your most frequent errand locations grouped together near your home or work for convenience: bank, dry cleaners, pharmacy, gas station, grocery store, car wash.
3. Keep a list of all errands that you need to do so that you will not forget something.
4. Grocery shop and run other errands at off-peak hours to avoid the crowds.

Invitations and Events

1. Have one calendar at home on which you note all invitations and other commitments for all family members.
2. Remind family members to enter all obligations on the calendar as soon as they know them.
3. Learn to diplomatically say no to the requests and commitments you do not have time for or do not enjoy.
4. Keep any invitations so that you know all the details, and note on the invitation that you have RSVP'd if required so that you will not wonder later whether you did so.
5. The day before an event at a location where you have not previously been, go online and check directions.

Mail, Magazines, and Catalogs

1. Open your mail at the kitchen trash bin and immediately toss junk mail and catalogs that you do not want rather than let them accumulate.
2. Shred any identifying information found in credit card offers or other junk mail (your airline frequent flyer number, a policy number for the offered insurance, a temporary membership card for roadside assistance).
3. If you receive catalogs, credit card offers, and coupons that you did not request, contact www.catalogchoice.org to have them stopped.
4. Discontinue any magazine subscriptions that you no longer wish to receive.
5. Ask a neighbor to collect your mail when you are out of town or stop your mail online with the U.S. Postal Service (currently mail can be held for no less than three days and no longer than three weeks).

Meals and Meal Preparation

1. Have dinner as a family each week at least two or three times for payoffs in communication, family unity, and understanding of your children.

2. Plan your dinner menus for the week and pull the recipes to check the preparation time and difficulty to determine which day to prepare a dish.
3. After choosing your menu for the week, list all ingredients that you will need to shop for ahead of time so that everything will be on hand.
4. When possible, assign meal preparation duties to family members for nights that would fit their schedules.
5. Make sure that the recipe and a list of helpful tips are set out in the morning with the ingredients easily accessible on the counter and in the refrigerator.
6. Complete as much food preparation on the weekends as possible.
7. Make several slow-cooker meals over the weekend for fast weekday meals.
8. When putting away groceries, place items on the shelves of the pantry and refrigerator using the FIFO system (first in, first out) so that older items are moved to the front and the newer items are moved to the back.
9. Once a month, go through your freezer and pantry to locate items with approaching expiration dates and plan those items into your menus.

Routines

1. Have one place at home to leave your keys, briefcase, and other office essentials to avoid hunting for them each morning.
2. Have other family members each have a place where they leave backpacks or other school and work essentials each evening for the same reason.
3. Get up a half hour or hour before anyone else in your family to give yourself quiet time to prepare for the day, have a cup of coffee, read the paper, and wake up.
4. Have regular routines that you follow each morning to prepare for the day and each evening to prepare for bed.

5. Check the weather forecast before you go to bed so that you will know whether you need to allow for extra commute time in the morning.

6. Lay out your wardrobe the night before to avoid the surprise of a missing button or unpolished shoes in the morning.

7. Fill lunch boxes with napkins, cutlery, and non-refrigerated essentials the night before and leave them on the kitchen counter.

8. Make sandwiches and package perishable lunch items the night before and place the items together in the refrigerator for quick packing of lunch boxes in the morning.

9. Leave ten minutes earlier than you may need for any destination so you will not be rushed.

10. Wait for the peak traffic times to pass before you start your commute whenever possible and find the window of time when there are fewer cars on the road.

11. Keep a book, magazine, or newspaper in your car so you will have something productive to do while you wait in standstill traffic on the freeway because of an accident or roadwork.

12. Schedule regular phone calls with family and friends for times that are convenient for you even though you should *not* announce that it is a scheduled time.

Appendix C:
Easy Ideas for Lowering Stress

1. Eat three nutritionally balanced meals a day at regular times.
2. Sleep seven to eight hours every night.
3. Go to bed and get up at the same time each day.
4. Exercise at least 150 minutes per week.
5. Lower your caffeine intake: chocolate, soda, tea, coffee.
6. Lower your sugar, alcohol, and junk food intake.
7. Drink plenty of water each day to stay hydrated.
8. Eat light snacks to renew your energy in the afternoon: a handful of nuts, a small box of raisins, a granola bar, a piece of fruit.
9. Take a fifteen-minute power nap in the afternoon when you are at home.
10. Stand up every hour and walk around for five minutes to take a mental break.
11. Take a short walk at lunch time.
12. Surround yourself with green plants to increase your oxygen intake.
13. Reserve one weekend a month that is completely unscheduled and can be used spontaneously however you feel at the time.
14. Volunteer for a community service project at least once a month to keep perspective on your life.
15. Make dinner for or eat out with friends several times a month.
16. Post motivational sayings throughout your home.
17. Have a ten-minute telephone conversation with someone you care about each day.
18. Go through old family photographs that will remind you of pleasant events in your life.
19. Surround yourself with positive and supportive people.
20. Read one inspirational quote or scripture each morning.
21. Each morning, list three blessings in your life—no matter how small.
22. Do one random act of kindness each day.

23. At the end of the day, remind yourself of three good things you did that day—no matter how small.
24. Keep a journal in which you write down only positive things: thoughts, happenings, and blessings. Reread entries once a month.
25. Say "please" and "thank you" more often.
26. Send a card to someone important to you with a handwritten note saying how much you value that person's friendship, support, or love.
27. Refuse to listen to gossip or start gossip.
28. Compliment someone on a project, item of clothing, or some other aspect.
29. Smile at yourself each time you pass a mirror or see your reflection in a door or window.
30. Read at least one book that is not related to law each month.
31. Put on upbeat music in the car and sing along.
32. Get a massage once a month.
33. Take a drive in the country to admire the scenery.
34. Find a good viewing spot to enjoy a sunset or sunrise.
35. Treat yourself to a frozen yogurt or ice cream cone once in a while.
36. Take a popcorn break.
37. Swim five lengths.
38. Run or play a racquet sport for thirty minutes.
39. Spend time in a sauna.
40. Spend time in a hot tub.
41. Laugh about something you did today.
42. Read a joke book for fifteen minutes.
43. Watch a funny TV program or movie.
44. Read a story to a child.
45. Play with a child for a half hour.
46. Giggle with a child about something silly.
47. Pet the family dog or cat.
48. Take your dog for a walk or a game of Frisbee.
49. Go for a leisurely walk in a park.

50. Watch the birds at a bird feeder.
51. Listen to a recording of a waterfall.
52. Get in touch with your spiritual side.
53. Do a guided imagery exercise to relax.
54. Do deep-breathing exercises to relax.
55. Do gentle shoulder rolls or neck rotations to relax muscles.
56. Do gentle stretching exercises when you get up in the morning.
57. Reward yourself for finishing major projects on time.
58. Keep a pad and pen on your nightstand; when you wake up concerned you will forget something, write it down and then go back to sleep without worry.
59. Spend ten minutes at least twice a day in silence without interruptions or distractions.
60. Relax in a room lit only by candles.
61. Listen to a CD of calming music.
62. Relax for a half hour before you go to bed.
63. Soak in a lavender bubble bath to induce sleep.
64. Drink warm milk and honey before bed to induce sleep.
65. Soak in a juniper bubble bath to decrease muscle stress.

Appendix D:
Relaxation Exercises

1. Close your eyes. Focus on your breathing. Breathe in deeply and exhale deeply. Count on each exhalation. Breathe in, exhale, one, breathe in, exhale, two, etc.

2. Close your eyes. Focus on your breathing. Breathe deeply. Repeat a positive word over and over to yourself. Relax your posture.

3. Rub your palms together very fast for a count of twenty. Lay your palms flat on the surface in front of you. Let them rise up very slowly as high as they will go. Let them drop slowly back to the surface. Repeat several times.

4. Rotate your neck gently and slowly to the right, back, left, forward. Repeat as your neck muscles relax.

5. Hold your neck in a centered and upright position with your face forward. Turn your head gently 90 degrees to the right. Return to center. Turn your head gently 90 degrees to the left. Return to center. Repeat as your neck muscles relax.

6. Roll your shoulders gently and slowly backward numerous times. Reverse and roll them forward.

7. Interlock your fingers and stretch your arms in front of you. Raise your arms with fingers interlocked and stretch them above your head. Return your arms to the position in front of you. Relax. Repeat.

8. Sit back in your chair. Stretch your legs out in front of you and hold them several inches above the ground. Point your toes upward. Gently rotate your feet in right circles together. Stop. Gently rotate your feet in left circles together. Relax.

9. Hold your right or left hand so that your palm is facing upward and flat. Knead your palm gently with the thumb of the other hand on top and the fingers of the other hand supporting the massaged palm underneath. Massage in a counterclockwise direction around the outside of the palm. If you find a tender or "crunchy" spot, massage slightly harder. Relax the rest of your body as you massage your palm.

10. Knead a stress ball in one hand. Switch hands and repeat. Relax.

11. Sit up straight. Scrunch your shoulders up toward your ears. Relax. Repeat.

12. Sit in a comfortable chair or lie down. Close your eyes. Relax. Now tighten the muscles in your toes. Relax them. Next tighten the other muscles in your feet. Relax them. Continue to tighten and then relax each muscle group in small increments all the way through your body to the top of your head. Relax completely for ten minutes. Open your eyes and get up.

13. Sit in a comfortable chair or lie down. Close your eyes. Picture a favorite scene (beach, forest clearing, country lane). Mentally walk slowly around the scene in your mind. Enjoy the sounds, smells, and sights. Savor the pleasure you had the last time you were in that location. Open your eyes.

Index

proactive handling of,
61–63
for research projects, 86
tips for, 179
for writing projects, 95
Decision-making power, 57
Delegation of tasks, 65–80
asking for assistance in,
69–71, 175
charts for, 78
choosing person for, 74
communication and
discussions, 75–77
evaluation of finished
product, 79
experience and willingness
for, 70–71
following-up on, 77–79
forms for, 38, 76, 77
steps for effectiveness in,
71–79
support staff relationship
and, 65–69
time considerations and,
74–75
tips for, 179–180
types of, 71–73
Desks. See Work surface
organization
Dictation, 19–21
Document handling
assembly software and
templates for, 5, 19, 180
electronic vs. paper, 4–5,
17

Dragon NaturallySpeaking
software, 21

E
Effectiveness, defined, 1, 24
Efficiency, defined, 1, 24
Electronic databases, 5, 83–86,
90
Electronic vs. paper
documents, 4–5, 17
E-mail, 108–117
appropriateness of,
110–111
archiving system, 116–117
confidentiality issues, 111
inbox organization,
114–116
minimizing interruptions
from, 109–110
overview, 108–109
research projects
presented in, 95–96,
95n1
rules and tips for, 113–114,
181–182
writing effectively in,
111–113
Employee benefits, taking
advantage of, 158
Employer policies and trends,
6–7, 46–47, 103, 158
Energy level considerations,
45–46, 187
Equipment and furniture in
office, 9–11, 12, 145, 182

Work management, *continued*
  office furniture and
    equipment, 9–11, 12,
    145, 182
  organization of work
    surfaces, 11, 13–17,
    14n1
  overview, 9
  physical workspace
    organization, 9–11, 12,
    143–146, 195–196
  tips. *See* Tips for
    better time and work
    management
Workspace organization, 9–11,
  12, 143–146, 195–196

Work surface organization, 11,
  13–17, 14n1
Writing projects, 91–95
  deadlines, 95
  editing and revision
    process, 93, 94
  initial drafts, 92–93
  interruptions, 93–94
  outline review, 92
  prewriting stage, 91
  reevaluation of research
    findings, 92
  tips for, 196–197

Y
Yearly task lists, 26–27

About the Author

Amy L. Jarmon is the Assistant Dean for Academic Success Programs and an Adjunct Professor at Texas Tech University School of Law. She teaches Introduction to Legal Studies, Comparative Law: English Legal System, and European Union: Institutions and Principles. She previously served as an Adjunct Professor, the Acting Assistant Dean for Law Student Services, and the Director of Academic Success Programs at The University of Akron School of Law.

She is a Co-Editor of the Law School Academic Support Blog and a regular contributor to *Student Lawyer*, the American Bar Association Law Student Division magazine.

In the United States, she has worked for the Supreme Court of Virginia, for a national law firm, and as a consultant for the Virginia Trial Lawyers Association. While living in the United Kingdom, she practiced law at two English law firms. She is admitted to practice in Virginia and is on the rolls as a Solicitor in England and Wales. She has both a law degree and a doctorate in higher education administration from The College of William and Mary.

Prior to her legal career, she served as a professional in student affairs for seventeen years at four colleges and universities, ending her career as a Dean of Students.